CHASTITY, POVERTY, AND OBEDIENCE

CHASTITY, POVERTY, AND OBEDIENCE

Recovering the Vision for the Renewal of Religious Life

by

MOTHER MARY FRANCIS, P.C.C.

IGNATIUS PRESS   SAN FRANCISCO

Original edition published under the title *Marginals*
© 1967 by Franciscan Herald Press, Chicago, Illinois
Published with ecclesiastical permission

New edition printed by permission of
The Community of Poor Clares of New Mexico, Inc.

Cover art: *Received by Saint Francis*
Detail from *St. Clare* with eight stories from her life
Anonymous, Thirteenth Century
S. Chiara, Assisi, Italy
Scala / Art Resource, NY

Cover design by Roxanne Mei Lum

ISBN 978-1-58617-119-3
Library of Congress Control Number 2005938826
Printed in the United States of America ∞

To

His Holiness

Pope Paul VI

with filial love and loyalty

CONTENTS

FOREWORD

The late Mother Mary Francis of the Poor Clare Monastery of Our Lady of Guadalupe at Roswell in New Mexico lived intensely the renewal of religious life, which was mandated by the Second Vatican Council's Decree *Perfectae Caritatis*, "On the Fitting Renewal of Religious Life" ["Decree on the Adaptation and Renewal of Religious Life"], promulgated on October 28, 1965. Having received an initial formation in the apostolic religious life from the School Sisters of Notre Dame, who had taught her at the historic and beloved Saint Alphonsus Liguori Parish in her hometown of Saint Louis, Missouri, Mother Mary Francis heard the call to enter a religious institute dedicated completely to contemplation. On July 7, 1942, she entered the Poor Clare Colettine monastery of the Immaculate Conception in Chicago. In 1948, she, together with seven other nuns of her monastery, was chosen to make a Poor Clare foundation at Roswell in New Mexico.

Mother Mary Francis was elected Abbess of the Monastery of Our Lady of Guadalupe at Roswell in 1964, an office that she exercised with the greatest distinction for over forty-one years. The vitality of the monastery at Roswell, from which six foundations have been made, is a testimony to the totally sound and profoundly loving governance of Mother Mary Francis. A most gifted writer,

Mother Mary Francis has left us an account of the foundation at Roswell in her classic, *A Right to Be Merry*, first published in 1956 by Sheed and Ward and republished in a new edition by Ignatius Press in 2001. *A Right to Be Merry* not only tells the story of the foundation at Roswell but, more importantly, describes, in a most accessible and engaging manner, the nature of the life of a religious dedicated completely to contemplation.

In 1997, Ignatius Press published *Forth and Abroad*, Mother Mary Francis' sequel to *A Right to Be Merry*, in which she gives an account of the first five foundations made from the Monastery of Our Lady of Guadalupe. In both volumes, the reader discovers a remarkable depth of reflection upon the consecrated life, especially as it is lived by contemplative nuns. Mother Mary Francis' reflection makes most evident her love of her vocation.

Mother Mary Francis not only loved her vocation but also had the gift of communicating to others the great gift of religious life, the gift of total espousal to Christ and, therefore, of total love of the Church and, indeed, of all mankind. As Mother expresses it so strikingly and well in chapter three of *A Right to Be Merry*, the walls of the monastic enclosure encompass the whole world with love.

The just-mentioned volumes are only two of a number of books written by Mother Mary Francis, which include not only reflections on the consecrated life but also meditations, poetry, and religious plays. In 2006, Ignatius Press published a new edition of her *But I Have Called You Friends*, the collection of her most inspiring and helpful conferences on Christian friendship. One of the most beautiful of Mother's plays is *Counted As Mine*, which presents the story of the apparitions and message of Our Lady of Guadalupe. First published by Samuel French in 1954, it was published again as an operetta in three acts, with the musical score of Father Joseph Roff, in 1961 by the Gregorian Institute of America and is available today through the monastery at Roswell.

Her study and writing were devoted, in a most special way, to the vocation and mission of Saint Francis of Assisi, Saint Clare of Assisi, and Saint Colette of Corbie. Regarding Mother Mary Francis, one of the nuns at Roswell has rightly observed: "Her exceptional love for our Holy Father Francis and Holy Mother Clare gave her a connaturality with them in living and understanding their ideal and form of life, which she freely embraced and chose with a sense of privilege, as one who considered herself unworthy of such a grace." Mother's study of the life of Saint Colette of Corbie, *Walled in Light: St. Colette*, is remarkable for the depth of its research and of its insight into the Providence of God at work for the reform of the Poor Clare discipline. Mother Mary Francis could rightly declare, as Saint Colette of Corbie had declared so many times: "I am only the servant of Sir Saint Francis and Madame Saint Clare."

I know well of what I write not only because I have been blessed to read the writings of Mother Mary Francis. After having exchanged correspondence with Mother Mary Francis, beginning in 1999, when I, as bishop of La Crosse, had the hope of a Poor Clare foundation from Roswell in my beloved home diocese, I met Mother, for the first time, in January of 2002. At Mother's invitation,

I made a three-day visit to the Poor Clare monastery at Roswell. Each year since January of 2002, I have visited the nuns at Roswell for three to four days. Meeting Mother Mary Francis and having many conversations with her and with the community of nuns in chapter, over the years, has been a source of the greatest inspiration to me as a bishop.

Mother Mary Francis was most pleased when, on December 2, 2003, I was transferred from the Diocese of La Crosse to become the archbishop of her home diocese, the Archdiocese of Saint Louis, of which she had so many fond memories. After my transfer, our conversations always included the subject of Saint Louis, especially of her home parish, Saint Alphonsus Liguori Parish, under the care of the Redemptorist Fathers for whom she had the greatest affection; of the School Sisters of Notre Dame who were her teachers at Saint Alphonsus Liguori School and from whom she received a first formation in the religious life; and of Saint Louis University of which she was a proud alumna. As she recounts in *A Right To Be Merry*, it was a Jesuit Father at Saint Louis University who assisted her in discerning her vocation. In short, the friendship I formed with Mother and her community has been and continues to be a singular and most treasured blessing in my life.

From 1965 to 1991, Mother Mary Francis served the Poor Clare Federation of Mary Immaculate, of which the Roswell monastery is a member, as federal abbess or first councilor. Both within her own monastery, in which she was serving as abbess at the time of the promulgation of *Perfectae Caritatis*, and in her visitations, as federal abbess, to other Poor Clare monasteries, Mother Mary Francis manifested the deepest love for the Church and a truly remarkable wisdom about the Holy Spirit's most delicate and esteemed gift of the contemplative form of consecrated religious life.

Indeed, contemplative communities throughout the world recognized Mother Mary Francis as an authoritative voice for the renewal of religious life, in accord with the teaching and discipline enunciated by the Second Vatican Council and the post-Conciliar legislation. Mother Mary Francis died on February 11, 2006, the memorial of Our Lady of Lourdes, almost sixty-four years from her entrance into the Poor Clare monastery at Chicago. On the following Saint Valentine's Day, the day on which she would have completed her eighty-fifth year of life, the Mass of Christian Burial was celebrated, and Mother was laid to rest in the burial vault of the monastery, within the enclosure from which she had poured out the love of Christ for the Church throughout the world.

Mother Mary Francis lived the charism of universal love, which is the mark of the contemplative religious vocation. She lived that life, according to the gift of the Holy Spirit given to Saints Francis and Clare of Assisi. She understood that the Holy Spirit's gift of the consecrated life in the Church, in the particular form in which it is conferred on each founder or foundress of a religious community, remains always the same, even when some fitting adaptation is made for the living of the vocation in a particular time and place.

With regard to such adaptation, she understood that the guarantee of the fittingness of the adaptation comes by way of the pastoral office of the Successor of Saint Peter, the Roman Pontiff. By her loyalty to the Church universal, expressed in obedience to the Bishop of the Universal Church, she guarded and fostered, with humility and confidence, the great gift of the Holy Spirit to the Church, which has come to us through Saint Francis and Saint Clare. In reading Mother's writings and in my conversations with her, I have frequently marveled at how naturally and lovingly she referred to Saints Francis, Clare, and Colette, as if she had lived with them and conversed with them. She knew them intimately and loved them.

Having lived the contemplative religious life for nearly two decades before the Second Vatican Council, and having received the responsibility of governing a monastery and providing leadership to a federation of monasteries during the time after the Council, Mother Mary Francis manifested both the wisdom of one who treasures the life of Christ as it is handed down to us in the Tradition and the courage of one called to live the life of Christ in the present and for the sake of the future.

As with other aspects of the teaching and discipline set forth by the Second Vatican Council, the Decree *Perfectae Caritatis* was misunderstood and misinterpreted by some who, in the name of applying the teaching and discipline it contained, cultivated disdain for the life of religious in the time before the Council and proposed a future for religious life that was a kind of complete break with what had been. Mother Mary Francis knew that it was not possible that the Holy Spirit, who had been giving the gift of contemplative religious life to Poor Clare

nuns over the centuries, had somehow been mistaken and
was now giving the gift in a completely different form.
Wisely, Mother knew that an approach to fitting renewal
could come only through a deep appreciation of the work
of the Holy Spirit in the religious community over the
centuries and fidelity to the continued promptings of the
Holy Spirit, in an unbroken line of grace from the first
inspiration of the founder or foundress.

*Chastity, Poverty, and Obedience: Recovering the Vision for
the Renewal of Religious Life*, originally published in 1967
by Franciscan Herald Press under the title *Marginals*, contains the wise reflections of Mother Mary Francis on
the text of *Perfectae Caritatis*, especially as it applies to the
vocation of the Poor Clare nuns. For example, at a time
when participation in workshops and seminars led by those
who had little or no depth of knowledge of the charism
of a particular religious institute along with the consul-
tation of various experts with a similar lack of knowledge and appreciation were held to be the sure way to
foster the renewal of the various aspects of religious life,
Mother Mary Francis did not hesitate to observe that
many of these approaches to renewal turned out to be
"mere long-ringing condemnations of the past".

Acknowledging that "mistakes have been made in the
past," Mother, in her acute and most charming way,
observed: "Let us go on from there, not hold a seminar
there." She reminded her sisters in Christ: "Let us by all
means get expert guidance in the areas just mentioned
[the formation of novices and juniors, the psychological
aspects of religious life, and mental hygiene] and many
others, the while not letting the fact elude us that the

Holy Spirit remains *the* Expert, *the* Counselor." In the mind of Mother Mary Francis, the fitting renewal of religious life consists in the changing of the expression of a truth which itself must remain unchanged. To make such changes of expression, "we must be absolutely sure of that truth and educated to deal with it."

Rightly, she understood that authentic renewal of religious life must have its inspiration and take its direction from the gift of the Holy Spirit, namely, the charism given to the religious institute, which is fundamentally always the charism of Christlike love. She wisely observed: "The religious in ardent pursuit of charity will work first of all and most energetically of all at an interior renewal of love, both welcoming new ideas and reverencing valid old ones." In her wisdom, Mother saw that the "interior renewal of love" would guarantee the "good sense" of the renewal. For Mother Mary Francis, the fitting renewal of religious life could not admit of a rupture between religious life as it was lived before the Second Vatican Council and the way it is lived today. If it did, it would not be the renewal but the corruption and eventual destruction of religious life.

Throughout her reflections on *Perfectae Caritatis*, Mother Mary Francis demonstrates how the teaching and discipline set forth by the Second Vatican Council leads the religious to an ever deeper knowledge and love of the gift of the Holy Spirit given to his or her religious institute at its foundation. The Council insisted that the fitting renewal of religious life must, at once, include both: (1) "the constant return to the founts of the whole Christian life and to the original inspiration of the institutes";

and (2) "their adaptation to the changed conditions of the times" (*Perfectae Caritatis*, no. 2). Commenting on no. 14 of *Perfectae Caritatis*, on obedience to superiors, for example, Mother Mary Francis declares: "'Medieval' Saint Clare condensed a workshopful of ideas on the accessibility, serviceability, and approachability of the superior in one sentence of her Testament: 'Let her also be so kind and courteous that they can confidently make known their needs and trustingly have recourse to her at any hour as it will seem to them profitable to do, both for themselves as for their sisters.'"

In conclusion, in accord with the humility and confidence manifested to a remarkable degree in her contemplative religious life, Mother Mary Francis sets forth, with a most accessible and reliable text, the teaching and discipline contained in *Perfectae Caritatis*. She demonstrates how the Council served so well the good of each individual religious institute, urging its members to a constant study of the original inspiration of the institute and to the faithful expression of the inspiration in our time. I wholeheartedly commend *Chastity, Poverty, and Obedience: Recovering the Vision for the Renewal of Religious Life* to all members of institutes of the consecrated life, and to all who seek a deeper understanding of the renewal of religious life in our time and all that it means for the Church throughout the world. According to the wisdom of the teaching of the Second Vatican Council, "[t]he more fervently, therefore, [religious] join themselves to Christ by this gift of their whole life, the fuller does the Church's life become and the more vigorous and fruitful the apostolate" (*Perfectae Caritatis*, no. 1).

Mother Mary Francis is an always reliable spiritual guide. Reading her commentary on *Perfectae Caritatis*, you will discover a woman who was indeed a bride of Christ, a woman who gave herself totally to Christ for love of him and of his Mystical Body, the Church. You will experience her love which, modeled on the love of the Mother of God, will lead you to Christ and to a more complete adherence to him in all things: "Do whatever he tells you" (Jn 2:5). Writing to her most loved sisters in her spiritual testament, Mother expressed the truth of her religious vocation, a truth which remains unchanged and unchanging, a truth which is a great source of blessing for the whole Church, for us all:

> "Cherish the Spouse of your hearts,
> cherish your vocation,
> and cherish one another.
> It is everything. I bless you.
> Your Mother."

The Most Reverend Raymond Leo Burke
Archbishop of Saint Louis
August 28, 2007
Memorial of Saint Augustine, Bishop and
    Doctor of the Church

I   *The Pursuit of Perfect Charity*

During the final session of the Second Vatican Council, Pope Paul VI and the Council Fathers were good enough to give us in the first two words of the Decree on the Adaptation and Renewal of Religious Life[1] an expression of the whole meaning of renewal and a sure guide for all our work of adaptation. "Perfectae caritatis", the Decree began. Perfect charity remains our norm for any past, present, or future implementation of the Council teaching, as well as our inspiration in working toward that goal. It is the prerequisite for any valid approach to adaptation, any examination of progress in our attempts at renewal. "The pursuit of perfect charity through the evangelical counsels ... reveals itself as a splendid sign of

[1] October 28, 1965.

I

the heavenly kingdom." When religious life is obviously not a splendid sign of the heavenly kingdom, or when it is a blurred or clouded sign, its basic deficiency is always that perfect charity is not being pursued.

True renewal begins within and issues outward. It cannot be exercised on externals in order to produce an interior effect. While it is very true that our interior lives are affected to a varying extent by externals, and we are foolhardy to maintain that we are not influenced by the aggression of outward circumstance and environment, still it remains true that renewal of religious life in any century is essentially an interior work. It is a work of love. And it is love alone that can give the vision needed to effect the outer renewal of life and discipline that is meaningful, productive of sanctity, and fruitful for all the people of God.

It is necessary to meditate more deeply on this "pursuit of perfect charity" in our efforts for the adaptation of religious life to modern times. Enthusiasm for changing externals was at high tide after the Council. And many externals clearly indicated the need for them to be modified or even entirely abrogated. However, it has never been possible to effect a better outward order if interior order has not first been examined and summoned before the judgment of the soul. "He has set charity in order within me" (Song 2:4). That we may have been running exuberantly in the wrong direction can be suspected by the general imbalance in the work of adaptation after the Council as, for example, change of religious garb so often being accorded first place. This has been a tragic usurpation of primacy. For the first place belongs to the love in the heart of the one wearing religious garb. And here the work of renewal must begin. What is the quality of that love? How comprehensive is it? How incisive is its vision? What is its capacity for giving? One used to hear many religious saying, "I'll be glad when we get the habit changed so that we can start to think about more important things." Could we not *have begun* with the "more important things" and thus had a clearer vision for discussing and deciding the less important things?

If we do not love enough, we shall always suffer from astigmatism in the work of renewal. If we do not love at all, we are totally unfit even to speak of proper adaptation. It is only when we love one another that we are capable of reverence for differing views. It is only the Christlike soul that has space in its chambers for the thought of others. And it is necessary that the religious woman be first a woman before she can be or even understand what it means to be a religious. The most painful phenomenon of our times could be that of religious who are vigorously introducing plans for better education of members, more involvement with people, more commitment to Christ in modern circumstances, but who are themselves uneducated in fraternal love, uninvolved in one another, uncommitted to the common ideal.

We have to enter deeply into the mystery of our own vocation before we can perform any surgeries on it. No matter how clearly surgery is indicated, the doctor first checks the heart rate of the patient and investigates the condition of his blood. And so the first clarion call of the Decree on adaptation and renewal is to the pursuit of perfect charity whereby alone religious life is shown for a splendid sign of the heavenly kingdom. Before we are a sign to all the people of God, we must first be a sign to one another. We shall never effect more good in the inner city than we do in the inner circle of the community or, more fundamentally, in the inner court of our own soul.

It was not the practice of perfect charity the Council had asked for, but the pursuit of it. Is there a trace of wonderful Godlike humor in this? A testimony to the weakness of our human condition? "See how they love one another!" pagans marveled at the first Christians who had worked so energetically at an interior renewal that their outward life was revealing itself for a splendid sign of the heavenly kingdom. Yet, as Father Thomas Worden once reminded us, these men and women, inflamed by the first Pentecostal "Council", often had a difficult time of it.[2] Peter and Paul differed angularly at times. Barnabas had to be reassigned to another mission band. Ananias and Saphira tried to make the best of both worlds. Paul, whom the charity of Christ "pressed", was moved to relieve his emotions by calling the high priest a "whitewashed wall". Love does need to be pursued. Charity is a lifetime study. Wonderfully, the very pursuit, the study itself, is a "splendid sign of the heavenly kingdom".

Thus it may be said that religious can be evaluated by what they are pursuing. If it is perfect charity, they will reveal this in the manner in which they discuss ideas, their openness to conviction, the gentleness with which

---

[2] *The Psalms Are Christian Prayer* (New York: Sheed and Ward, [1961]), pp. 117ff.

they handle the ideas of others. If they are pursuing phantoms of mere external change without striving for any true interior renewal and reflowering of charity, this will be only too clearly manifested by the intolerance, condescension, and contradictiveness that characterize their "dialogue" with others. There is sometimes an amusing spirit of monologue in those who plead most impassionedly for the need of dialogue. Dialogue does not properly mean either myself endorsing my own opinions or my first lieutenant applauding my ideas.

The great impetus given to discussion by Vatican II provided us with an extraordinarily fine self-revelatory device. Maybe our greatest personal discovery was that of our ineptitude in the art of listening—or our pet fixation, or our dearest bias. The tendency to reject a new idea has been a longtime hazard for some nuns. The tendency to reject all old ideas is a modern hazard for some other nuns. For a religious to indulge either tendency is for her to cease being a splendid sign of the heavenly kingdom because it is to have ceased actively pursuing perfect charity that both "casts out fear" (1 Jn 4:18) and ensures proper perspective. "Disregard tradition, and the past will come back and bury you", remarked Shane Leslie, with enviable perspicacity. The religious in ardent pursuit of charity will work first of all and most energetically of all at an interior renewal of love, both welcoming new ideas and reverencing valid old ones. It is love alone, in the end, that makes for good sense.

The response to the summons to adaptation in religious life with a sizzle of ideas for shortening the skirts, demolishing the refectory lecterns, enlarging the swimming pools, and melting down the bells was not the answer the Decree *Perfectae Caritatis* solicited. This is not to disclaim any shortening of skirts or to deplore the swimming pool. It is only to maintain that renewal must begin within and work outward. It is to express the conviction that an adaptation concerned only with externals is a spurious adaptation. In such misdirection may lie part of the explanation of why external "adaptations" and defections from religious life have kept pace very nicely. What is born of thoughtful love is in turn fecund with holiness; it will endure. The pursuit of perfect love indicates where and how changes are to be made. Conversely, the pursuit of change does not posit love.

Perfectae Caritatis states, "Indeed from the very beginning of the Church men and women have set about following Christ with greater freedom and imitating Him more closely through the practice of the evangelical counsels" (no. 1). This is what we must educate our young members to appreciate: that vows are means of following Christ with greater freedom. It is a betrayal of youth to present it with a superficial concept of freedom. The liberty to be a churl, to whimper when we are misunderstood, to defy authority if we are crossed, to equate our own wishes with the will of God but to reject any equation of the superior's directives with the will of God, to make the development of our talents (real or imaginary) the end of our endeavors—these aspects of "liberty" are within the reach of all, but are scarcely to be prized. "Following Christ with greater freedom and imitating Him more closely", reads the Decree. No one was ever so misused as Christ, no one so rejected, no one's "talents" so little used, no man ever so victimized by the very shabbiest specimens of authority. Yet it is because Christ humbled himself and obeyed unto death that the Father has exalted him and given him a name above all other names (see Phil 2:8–9).

Freedom to express themselves, freedom to contribute to the immediate religious community and to the large community of the people of God, freedom to be individual persons with an individual work to do for God: these are delineations of freedom we want to make clear and accessible to our members in both initial and ongoing formation. But we must educate them to a more profound understanding of freedom than just this. We must help them to enter into the mystery of Christ, whose behavior and evaluations would be considered by some current standards as very odd. In modern language, we might put it this way: that it was precisely when Christ could not get his ideas across and was frustrated by small-minded persons in authority who could not see past their phylacteries, when he was quite literally slapped down to his "proper place", that he redeemed us. Not every kind of peace is the peace of Christ: "*My* peace I give you" (Jn 14:27). Not all concepts of freedom are his concepts of freedom. The "liberty of the children of God" is a tremendous and very taxing condition to be in or even to aspire toward.

"The more fervently, then, they are joined to Christ by this total life-long gift of themselves, the richer the life of the Church becomes and the more lively and successful its apostolate." What a sentence that is! It must be giving, and giving until death do us part, soul and body.

It must be total, not surplus peelings off self but the core and the marrow. And it must be a gift of "themselves", not merely a donation of energy or a settlement of capabilities.

Entering religious life is not a matter of opening a bank account in the Church wherein we deposit our talents and demand interest on them. We must become freer and freer to give more and more, practically aware of the ancient paradox that the less we give, the less we have; and the more we squander ourselves on God, the more we have left to bestow. "Those who do things for their own maturity and development are the everlasting adolescents in religious life", Father Bernard Häring, C.Ss.R. once remarked. We want to be absorbed with giving, not with getting. It is by giving totally, perpetually, radically, that we enrich the life of the Church and make her apostolate lively and successful.

Christ's ideas of success as evidenced in his life and death, our perfect model, compare very strangely sometimes with our ideas of success. For him, success was to give, utterly, sufferingly. He "got" very little out of his human life as we consider "getting". True, when dear Peter asked what he was going to get out of this thing, out of his splendid giving of some torn fishnets (the Scriptures tell us they had to be mended) and a not-too-seaworthy craft (see Mk 4:35–41, the storm on the waters), Christ did pledge a reward for giving. However, he did not promise to send Peter to piscatorial college to develop his skills and return him as the most professional fisherman in Galilee. "What shall we have, if we give?" "A hundredfold in this life, and eternal happiness in the next"

(Mk 10:30). And what is the hundredfold if not to find a hundredfold manner to give? This seems to have been how it functioned in Peter. And eternal happiness? For this we wait with expectant hearts, as we enrich the Church and enliven her apostolate by our total giving of ourselves, each new day again.

II   *Two Directions*

In our work of renewal, it is more than religious for all seasons that the Church urges us to be. She makes it plain that we must be religious of two directions. To look in two directions, and more especially to *move* in two directions, is less a matter of a charism than of an acquired art. While it is not a happy condition of life that a religious be running in all directions, it is needful for an intelligent approach to adaptation that a religious be able to move in two directions, backward and forward. In the present preoccupation with self-development, the tending of this talent for bilateral spiritual vision and movement may sometimes be neglected.

Vatican Council II has urged us all to go forward. But in the Decree *Perfectae Caritatis*, it reminds us that we cannot properly go forward unless we look backward, nor soar upward if we do not plunge downward. Neither will it be sufficient to do this once. "The adaptation and renewal of the religious life includes both the constant return to the sources of all Christian life and to the original spirit of the institutes and their adaptation to the changed conditions of our time" (*Perfectae Caritatis*, no. 2; hereafter abbreviated as PC). A *constant* return. How much of the Church's ageless wisdom inflames that word; how much of her awareness of the stuff of which her children are made! "He knows what we are made of; he remembers that we are but dust" (Ps 103 [102]:14). So does the Church. She exhorts us to remember that if our efforts to proclaim a new message of religious life do not gather their strength from and discover their character in the original purpose of our religious life and the spirit of our founder, we shall only be carrying dust against the wind.

It must always be for us not a task of discovering the past, but of constantly recovering it. Only in this continual repossession of a heritage shall we be able to determine the best means of presently dispensing its riches, both to our own inner selves and to all the people of God. Before we can adapt anything "to the changed conditions of our time", we obviously have to be conversant with unchangeables. To strike bottom bedrock, we could put it this way: that we have to understand what we are changing before we can availingly change it. Similarly, we have to love with a knowledgeable love what we are changing if we are not to deface or even to mutilate it. It is invigorating to run forward and let the wind whistle in one's ears; but a race presupposes a starting point and it has a goal. To run for the mere exhilaration of running is a sport that palls in a very short time. Too long pursued, it precipitates heart attacks or total collapse—which is to say: crisis or abandoning one's vocation.

In urging a constant return to the sources of all Christian life and the original spirit of the institute, Vatican II was putting only a single obligation on Franciscans: the Gospels, in the form of their Rule. This is for Franciscans not so much a matter of an equation as of a synonym. "The form of life of the Order of the Poor Sisters which the blessed Francis founded is this: to observe the holy Gospel of our Lord Jesus Christ", says Saint Clare in her Rule, which is simply a sustained echo of the Rule of Saint Francis.

Francis was a renovator, a radical, a reformer. He was so effective in these roles because he understood what he was renewing, respected the roots without which plants cannot live, and knew that there cannot be reformation without a knowledge of and love for the original formation. He always went back to the Gospels. He always returned to Christ. That is why he was able to press forward with strength and purpose. He never betrayed the people of God by having only Francis to give them. He brought them Christ. And he did this so effectively that his message and his burden were unmistakeable to both the learned hierarchy of his time and the unlettered country folk. They called him "the Christ of Umbria".

We cannot hope to express, much less to be, the Christ of Los Angeles or the Christ of Springfield, the Christ of the ward, the classroom, or the cloister, unless we are steeped in our sources (his Gospel), and in our Source (himself). We can be availingly original only in the measure that we are imitators of Christ. We bear authentic witness to our times best when we bear it as Francis our father did—by witnessing to Christ. In this same way, we shall reinvigorate a blasé world with the freshness of Franciscan spirituality only insofar as we have drunk from the wellsprings of Franciscanism. Our era will become a wonder and not a horror according to the skill with which it puts new flesh on the strong sinews of source and origin.

The Church wants to strive in her outward forms to return to the simplicity of early Christianity, but without sacrificing anything of the intellectual, cultural, and even cultic developments of the centuries, even as she prepares herself for the future by identifying herself with the present. In returning to a source, we do not retrace our path to recover a modus operandi but an inspiration. In religious adaptation we do not want to study the original spirit of our institute with an architectural eye so as to continue to reproduce a given style, but with an architectural heart so that we rediscover the dream that was in the heart of the builder and learn to reproduce it with different building materials and perhaps even in a different style.

Twenty-first-century Franciscan attempts to imitate Saint Francis literally in those manifestations of his ideal that had a proper setting in the thirteenth century will end at best in caricature, at worst in apostasy. We can, in fact, become so bemused by the manifestations of an ideal that we fail to understand the ideal itself, or at least fail to distinguish the one from the other. It can be the subtlest of self-deceptions to work at reproducing in ourselves the mode and manner of the founder while neglecting to restate the spirit that produced through him an appropriate contemporaneity of mode and manner, producing in us an appropriate but necessarily different contemporaneity. It can even be merely another manifestation of the weakness that fights the spirit of the law with its own letter.

We shall not, for example, witness to the spirit of Francis today by not handling money because Francis refused to handle money. We could, however, offer the people of God a wonderfully "disconcerting" witness to the spirit of Francis by unwinding ourselves from our comforts and conveniences. He was such a hard realist, that little man who shook the thirteenth century with his presence. He knew how love of riches enervated men, so he simply put his two hands behind his back and steadfastly refused to "get the feel" of it. He insisted on preserving holes in all his pockets. Perhaps our greatest need in our struggle to delineate a present Franciscan witness to poverty is simply to have holes in our pockets—to relax a little our grasp on things, to leave off being proprietors of created goods and thus become their lord, as Francis was.

It is not so much what Francis did that we need to do, as it is who Francis was that we need to be. He was so realistic because he was so simple. He was so simple because he believed God. In an age that loves above all to look at itself in a hand mirror and whisper, "How adult!" it may cause some squirming on chairs and polite coughing behind hands to touch on the subject of childlikeness. Yet, a sophisticated spirituality will stub its pedicured toes not only on Francis, but on Christ. "Unless you be converted and become as little children . . ." (Mt 18:3).

Is not the explanation of why some of us grow so annoyed at the concept of "child" in religious life, why we take sternly to task those who use this term, that we have failed to plumb the meaning or even to recognize the mystery in Christ's unequivocal requirement for entrance into his kingdom? Not "unless you *are* as little children", but "unless you *become* as little children". Our Lord talks of a "conversion", advising us that we must undergo a change of belief and opinion, that we must readjust and rectify our sense of values if we are to have part at all with him. The divine Master tells us plainly that there is work to be done; he tells of a process of *becoming*. And in such a metamorphosis, there is always involved the arduous and the painful.

The apostles were still not free of their complicated ideas about the expected millennium, their ambitious bickerings, their very "adult" ideas about a triumphal Messiah when Christ called them his "little children". But he was trying to convert them. And they were in the process of becoming. Thus he would honor them with this affectionate title of distinction. When we grow distressed over the idea of a superior calling a novice "my child", we betray ourselves as unrealistic about the kingdom of the spirit, forgetting that it was grown men with hairy arms and smelling of fish and sweat whom Christ called his "little children", and that it was to men of age and able to speak for themselves (as well as to show ready evidence of ability to sin for themselves) whom fiery Paul sought to win for the Kingdom with the tender invitation "my little children".

True, we can embarrass and even destroy the noble spiritual concept of "child"; we can evade the responsibility entailed in seeking such clear vision by distorting the idea of "child" into a kind of infantilism. This is indeed tragic failure. But distortion of idea indicates only a deficiency in the distorters and not a defect in idea. We cannot live in this wonderfully challenging era of renewal like irresponsible singers among the daisies, but we can make our renewal more effectual and ensure its validity by approaching and executing it with the uncompromising vision of the child and all his taste for basic verities. Even the child's eternal question, why? can be our norm. If we do not know why we are currently doing or have been doing certain things, then we must either discover the valid reason and do these things intelligently or we must face the fact that if a reason once existed, it no longer does, and so put away these things. Similarly, if we wish to change things, it is required that we can answer, why?

One evidence of spiritual adulthood is the capacity for becoming like a child. It is a very difficult business to become as a little child, taking God at his word, believing our Father, trusting the will that we cannot fathom, and understanding, among other things, that it is only love that will effect any kind of valid renewal in anything.

This was the kind of child Saint Francis was. His simple holiness was his greatness as well as the secret of such a power over others as the world has not seen excelled. This is the spirit of the founder to which we are urged by Vatican Council II to return. Francis was a hard realist. That is why he was so great a poet. He never escaped down words or even ideas, but pursued them to an ultimate meaning. The dreamer-saint of Assisi was a man of such action as to happily upset a whole European society by his humble presence. Like all great dreamers, he got things moving. In fact, he got things done—and by the very simple expedient of doing them. He was first of all himself what he invited others to be. Surely there is no need to discuss Francis' witness to Christ in the Church before all the people of God. It is not a matter of the means of giving witness that he chose. He simply was himself a witness by his personal holiness.

So it must be with us. Society asks us with particular insistence these days to give an account of ourselves. But the account men really demand is that we show ourselves persons who know God intimately, live for him utterly, and are thus able to make the reality of the living God "come alive" for them also. They have every right to demand this account of us, and we have every duty to respond. It was the way of Saint Francis to speak to men simply, and always more by the caliber of his life than by his words, of a God he knew and loved and lived for. It was thus that he brought back to a languid and sensual society the enthusiasm and joy of the children of God.

With all the wonderful new avenues of theological speculation, the new scholarly exegeses, the reformed liturgy, the new concept of collegiality, and all the rest, it remains true that personal holiness alone will renew the Church. It has always taken saints, not scholars, to effect a true spiritual renewal. It always will.

In our efforts to resolve our identity crisis, whether as individuals or as an Order, Franciscans have the inspiration of a founder who knew exactly who he was. "I am the herald of the great King." If it was an appropriately medieval title for him, it is still a presently meaningful one for us. After all, Francis was only identifying himself as the *keryx* (herald) each of us must be. And he called out the kerygma less by his discourses than by his person, witnessing in words but witnessing more truly in being.

We are acutely concerned these days with the problem of relevancy. The facts that so many prelates in Saint Francis' day were avaricious, venal men; that so many devotees of pilgrimages and relic-collecting were cruel to their servants and licentious in their sexual relationships; that the "pious" were often the most crafty and cunning— these show clearly enough that relevancy is not a specifically modern problem. Making the Church relevant to man's daily life, making the Gospels relevant to the large and small business of human existence will always, in the end, reduce to personal holiness. Souls who are prepared by faith to meet God in the silence of prayer, there to discover what his love asks of them, and thence to surrender themselves completely to that love, these are the ones on whom the real and lasting work of renewal depends.

To meet God in faith, to surrender absolutely to his love is within the scope of each one, whether in friary or cloister, classroom or surgery or jungle. This is the whole secret of why Saint Francis in his simple way made the Gospel suddenly very relevant to men and emerged as the man of the pope's dream who held up the tottering Church with his own shoulder.

To emulate him in theory but not in practice is only a new version of pharisaism. Francis possessed nothing. For him, this meant very literal privations like eating crusts

and drinking water in company with disgruntled Brother
Masseo when he, quite as much as Masseo, appreciated
beef and wine. He was the great Christian existentialist.
He was a far better kind of empiricist in his simplicity
than we are in our sophistication. Francis was not afraid
to experience the things we are sometimes merely glib
about. Taking the beggar's place with his cup and in his
rags, Francis was the forerunner of all work in the inner
city. He was disconcertingly realistic about poverty. For
him it could only mean identification with the poor.

It would not be in a presently theatrical display of begging bread at the neighbors' doors that we would show
the first spirit of the Order today, but it is perfectly and
practically possible to adapt this idea "to the changed conditions of our time". If it is necessary to have our institutions furnished and equipped according to the required
standards of modern professionalism, it is still not necessary to be a prince in one's cell. It is less quaint than it is
sincere to guard against wastefulness. It would scarcely
evince a sense of realism or practicality to leave a lecture
hall, enthusiastic over an impassioned discourse on poverty in the modern world, only to consign to the caf-
eteria garbage disposal the selected expensive dessert from
which we have eaten two spoonfuls. These are very simple things, the kind of things that children understand.
They may warn us that we are becoming so "adult" as to
miss the point that a child clearly sees, and that he points
out, usually in an embarrassingly piercing voice and before
company.

"It redounds to the good of the Church that institutes have their own particular characteristics and work.

Therefore let their founders' spirit and special aims they set before them as well as their sound traditions—all of which make up the patrimony of each institute—be faithfully held in honor" (PC, no. 2b). A sound tradition of realistic, identifying love belongs to Franciscans. A son or daughter of Francis is never so much estranged from the spirit of the founder as when he does not love in this identifying manner. Saint Francis always wanted to experience the pain of others, the beggar, the leper, and—in his prayer on Mount Alverna—the redeeming Christ. He always wanted to see things just as they were. We are still putting up Christmas cribs in churches and homes in our own century because back in the thirteenth Francis wanted "to see how it was". He promoted among his sons "an adequate knowledge of the social conditions of the times they [lived] in and of the needs of the Church" (see PC, no. 2d), simply by entering into them. The Church of the thirteenth century needed to purify herself of triumphalism, of riches, of splendid trappings. So, instead of attacking the Church, Francis was himself poor. Lepers were despised and avoided. So, instead of belaboring society, Francis himself sought them out and washed them and cared for them—and so with other conditions, with other needs. It was a terribly realistic approach he had. To return to the original spirit of his institute, to his "spirit and special aims" (PC, no. 2b), demands that we *become* as little children—because we are not.

"The purpose of the religious life is to help the members follow Christ and be united to God through the profession of the evangelical counsels. It should be constantly kept in mind, therefore, that even the best adjustments made in accordance with the needs of our age will be ineffectual unless they are animated by a renewal of spirit. This must take precedence over even the active ministry" (PC, no. 2e). There is that "constantly" again! And there is a statement as simple as the heart of Saint Francis. The Council Fathers have warned us that the best outward adjustments will avail nothing without an interior renovation. And so in the work of renewal we must look first into our own hearts and let the difficult work of personal cleansing and uncluttering hold precedence.

III   *The Art of Listening*

Religious who are sincerely at work at the business of interior renovation will be religious receptive to the ideas of others and thus equipped to take their part in that "effective renewal and adaptation [which] demands the cooperation of all the members of the institute" (PC, no. 4).

It may be necessary to recall to ourselves that cooperativeness is not an infused virtue but an acquired skill sometimes hard won. For everyone, its acquisition will entail such predictable hardships for fallen human nature as the practice of humility and meekness. For some, the acquisition will call for spiritual yeomen's work. But Vatican II is quite unequivocal about declaring that there will be no effective renewal or adaptation without this full cooperation. Superiors need not only to evoke cooperation among their members, but to practice it themselves in their relations with their communities. While cooperation already defines itself etymologically as the work of all together, it devolves in a special way upon the superior. It would be something of a tragedy for *her* to think herself exempt from what it is her duty to promote: the working of all together.

Our generation specializes in discussion. But whether we are specialists at it is a question we shall have to ask ourselves. The two are not the same. It might be helpful to investigate some of the hazards in group discussions, dangers that either produce a tiresome sputtering-out of energies or, much more insidiously, render an apparently vital and animated discussion completely ineffective. Perhaps the commonest of such hazards is a deficiency in the art of listening.

More effective for the death of a discussion than the grosser expedients of interruption, contradiction, or floor holding, is the simple mental tuning out of views that do not coincide with our own. One could venture the opinion that it is better to be argumentive when one's personal views are challenged than impervious to challenge. Most of us prefer a hothead to a highhead. To listen requires humility, for the thesis basic to listening is that others may quite possibly have something of value to say, something from which we can profit. It presupposes a belief that I have not cornered the market on ideas. It retires me from the rostrum to the student assembly.

The art of listening is essential to the musician, the poet, the scientist. It is absolutely requisite to the Christian. And if the attitude of the learner and the listener is proper to all religious, it ought to be particularly characteristic of the Franciscan religious. Without it, family resemblance to the little seraphic listener of Assisi will be difficult to recognize. Saint Francis listened to God, to the Church, to his peers, to his subordinates. He became so adept in the art of listening that he even set up communication with lower creation. He was "for the birds" in a decidedly different sense than we give to the phrase today. Francis was, in fact, "for everybody" and was able to be so precisely because he listened to everybody, just as he listened to everybody because he was for everybody. In the end, one of the most respectable Franciscan legends gives us to understand, he even spoke Wolf rather well. Surely he is an inspiration for us who may not be empowered by God to tame ravening wolves but who may still be able to fill up a heartening measure both of ecumenism and of inner-circle understanding by learning to listen to and to learn from growls that, after all, are not specific to quadrupeds.

Radical to any availing renewal or adaptation is attentiveness to God. Invoking the Holy Spirit is not an accepted prefatory Church usage in the sense of being a routine hors d'oeuvre before the practical menu of affairs. Maybe we need to consider this, to be realistically and practically conscious of our need to be led, guided, and inspired by God. In an age of much professional counselling, the Holy Spirit remains the Paraclete, the Counsellor. Francis of Assisi had his own future neatly mapped out, his course all charted. He became a universal and enduring figure as *Saint* Francis rather than fading out historically as a small-town knight of no extrafamilial

significance to anyone, primarily because he learned how
to listen to God and to shape his life by God's instruc-
tions, even though this entailed a complete reshaping of
his own ideas and plans.

A superb listener, as superiors are presently warmly
(and sometimes heatedly) encouraged to be, Francis also
provides inspiration in another area where they are currently urged to operate: the risk area. After listening to
God and taking counsel, Saint Francis was willing to risk
making a mistake. He was not afraid to do the wrong
thing so long as he was honestly trying to do the right
thing. He knew that God is adept at bringing divine success out of human failure, and Francis was always prepared to do the best he could in the way he understood
it, not being the type of man to spend his whole life
taking barometric pressures and waiting for the proper
weather conditions in which to turn in a flawless performance. His faith and energy created its own weather.
In the end, he created a whole new climate for Europe
in the latter Middle Ages, and even penetrated the Orient.

When the voice of God told Francis to "go and rebuild
my Church which is falling into ruins", the saint listened carefully and heeded the voice. That he got the
message all wrong was not only all right, but has given
the rest of us meditation "material" for our lifetime. There
is field for piquant speculation on the divine humor of
God beholding Francis stumbling along with his stones,
sweating and straining, singing betweentimes, "rebuild-
ing the Church". There are few things more lovable in a
superior than his well-intentioned and admitted mistakes.
Similarly, there is at times something almost detestable in

the cautiousness of the worldly prudent who may never do anything right because they are too afraid that they may do something wrong.

It is only when superiors strive to be virtuoso listeners to God that they will be equipped to "take counsel in an appropriate way and hear the members of the order in those things which concern the future well being of the whole institute" (PC, no. 4). What is "an appropriate way"? Is it not a manner apropos to others, rather than to oneself? Here we touch on the second hazard of group discussions, though we shall want to say more about the first. It is the danger that the superior may be, and quite indeliberately, achieving the unhappy paradox of freezing a discussion by the warmth of her own views.

This danger will be most imminent in a united and happy community. It will be a perennial threat to the community situation in which the superior is as warmly loved as she is deeply respected. Religious, particularly religious women, may have less difficulty in responding to the summons for free opinions with complete candor when they feel personally remote from the superior than when they have a great affection for her. The superior who is fortunate enough to have a loving and devoted community must take particular pains to foster openness. It may be necessary for her to withhold her own opinion on certain points until she has heard the opinions of her sisters, not because they are immature children unable to form independent opinions or to pass personal judgments, nor again because their affection for her has created a hothouse atmosphere and one in which all the plants are vines, but for the simple and wholesome reason that we are all influenced in our judgments by regard for those we love, and the most spiritually refined are usually so influenced the most.

Wholesome, not weak, is the attitude, for example, of the superior who adjusts her plans, tempers her ideas, and delays certain objectively desirable actions to accommodate the spiritual and intellectual condition of the community. "He dawned upon the people, he did not take them by storm", writes Caryll Houselander of Christ. However, the superior must still be at pains to see that love's natural deference does not degenerate into intellectual paralysis. A strong-minded and warmhearted superior may naïvely suppose that she is affording her community an opportunity for frank and open discussions of customs, revisions, or some other area of adaptation and renewal, when actually she is only providing an opportunity for the sisters to tell her all the reasons she is right. Likewise, the sisters can become almost totally unaware that they are really not thinking at all, but only waving flags for the status quo. There may, happily enough, be excellent reasons for cheering a particular status quo at the moment, but we ought never to do this automatically, much less by reflex. Do we not all know something of the situation where a group discussion amounts to the superior saying, "This is what we have always done", and the community crying, "Hurrah!" and the superior saying, "This is what we shall go on doing", and the community responding with cheers? "Hurrah" is a delightful vernacular form of "alleluia", and the oftener it can validly be cried in a community, the better. But it must be an intelligent response, not a reflex grunt.

If a superior is aware of this kind of hazard in group discussions, she can ensure against the sisters becoming ditto marks either of herself or of one another by insisting that they give reasons for their views. If she gives out a list of points for discussion beforehand, it would be better not just to ask, "What do you think about this?" but to query, "*Why* do you think so?" Not "Should this common act of penance be retained?" but "*How* do you consider this penance to be effective right now?" or "*Why* is it ineffective?" Not "Should we abolish this usage?" but "What place do *you* feel this usage has in our communal witness to Christ? Could it be revitalized?"

Similarly, she could give practical testimony of her sincere openness to suggestion and prove the accessibility of her judgmental listening talents by sometimes expressing her pleasure that her sisters have been able to change her opinions by the excellence of their invited judgments and the validity of their reasoning. If in these and other ways she honestly labors to create and maintain an open atmosphere, she will not only be able to exercise her listening powers to her own and the community's great advantage, but will receive the happy reward of witnessing the suicide of criticism.

When religious have pragmatic proof and existential knowledge that their intelligent and respectfully submitted opinions are always and truly welcomed by the superior, even though it is to be understood that she may not always be able to accept them or act on them, there is simply no reason to be critical, except in the case of the unhappy few who have become addicted to criticism as a permanent mode of self-expression. However, more insidious than the mentality that impels a superior to bring down a verbal fist on all whom she considers nonconformists is the kind of closed-mindedness that cannot seriously envision the possibility of contrary opinions, or at least of their having any worth.

It is beyond question that there are today superiors who are serenely sure they have the pulse of their communities, whereas they actually have the pulse of only one section of the community. We may think we know the mind of our whole community—did we not give everyone every chance to speak her mind?—when, not having allowed for the type of mind that is especially susceptible to paralysis because of timidity, we actually do not know the mind of quite a number and might be amazed if we did.

The hazard for the timidly silent in a group discussion is often created more by a vehemently outspoken few than by the superior. Who has not witnessed discussions in which two or three jeeps devour the little Volkswagens on the first half mile? It is a very good thing to have strong opinions. It is an excellent thing, however, to be able to express them in an "I look at it this way" manner rather than in a "This is the way it is" fashion. It is a very practical possibility that a small group of persons will give an impression of a united opinion simply because there are too many mere auditors in the group and silence is accepted as consent, whereas it is actually sometimes impotent disagreement. And sometimes no one would be more surprised to discover that this silence is *not* consent than the vigorous "speakers". The art of listening has nothing to do with paralysis.

It is imperative that the superior rectify situations like this if we are to have really functional group discussions that avail for the "future well being of the *whole* institute" (PC, no. 4; emphasis added). She can do this in several ways. One is to draw out the views of the timid beforehand in personal interviews, and then herself create an opening wedge for them in the group discussion. A simple "What about looking at it this way?" from the superior during the meeting can be a kind of "sacramental" for a reticent sister unable to make her own wedge, but able to function and contribute in the wake of such charity.

"What about looking at it this way?" The superior herself may not see it this way at all, but she clears a path for the timid who do and who often have a surprising contribution to make once they are empowered to make it. Such a method is not to form a discussion but only healthily to condition it in favor of the retiring, who are not temperamentally equipped to fend for themselves in this region. The superior ought also to make it a point to provide as many soapboxes at a discussion as there are religious present. Some she will even have to give a helping hand to mount the thing. The leapers she may occasionally have to help down.

If there is an unfairness to religious in their not being able for one reason or another to express their opinions in a group discussion, this situation has another dimension of unfairness. It is in the direction of the superior who thinks she knows the mind of her community, but does not.

Saint Francis went to some lengths to draw out the timid, as is witnessed in the case of Brother Rufino. That he was willing to accept the counsel of his brothers to the very realistic extent of changing his mind appears repeatedly in his life. While the incident of the meal with Saint Clare is rejected by some scholars as legendary, its persistence in Franciscana seems to indicate truth by allegory if not by actuality. We are told that Francis, determined not to be a party to the repast, heard the voice of his friars and then himself made a decision, which was to follow their advice. It is a significant comment on the saint, too, that the friars showed no hesitation in speaking their views to him. One who considers it a weakness in authority to admit a change of opinion shows that she is very unsure of herself, her sisters, and her position.

To be jealous of an authority image is already to be unqualified to be a servant, which is what a superior is meant to be. Saint Francis never changed his ideals, but he rather frequently changed his mind. And he was much given to seeking counsel, from God in prayer, from the Scriptures, from his companions. Although we sometimes tend to confuse our ideals with our ideas, the two are definitely not the same. Perhaps we might even say that loyalty to ideals is best serviced by openness to new ideas. It can happen that a stubborn tenacity to our opinions, coupled with a convenient deafness to the views of others, testifies to the basic unsureness of our own position. If we are really certain of the validity of our stand, why do we arch our mental backs when it is questioned?

There are few things more frustrating in life than talking to a person who is determined not to listen, who may even have a sense of dedication to nonlistening. And how much is lost because of such situations! We can always learn something from our opponents, provided only we know how to listen. If nothing else, we can at least learn to suffer patiently with Christ, and this is already a tremendous service toward the "well being of the whole institute".

It is unfortunate that the very group discussions that are destined to dissolve tensions and strain, to promote open-mindedness, are instead sometimes remarkably successful in erecting tensions and strain and in manifesting closed-mindedness. Where this is unwillingness to listen, one may suspect that what purports to be firmness is actually merely stubbornness. And stubbornness is only a highly specialized form of weakness.

No normal person likes to be mistrusted. We may need to assess the caliber of our discussions to discover whether we are not so woefully deficient in tact at times as to give the impression that we consider any opinion other than our own a direct assault on the good of religion. Certainly there is much to deplore in certain current writings on the religious life, and one can scarcely be impressed by the splendid logic of certain modes of "thought" enjoying an ephemeral popularity at present. But surely we need not patrol our own opinions like a rifle-bearing sentry in the circle of community discussions. Such an attitude can all too easily degenerate into sarcasm, which is the language of immaturity, and eventuate in something akin to harangue. It would be a happy service to clean out the verbal snipers' nests in many papers and periodicals today and replace them with adult discussion columns. In the measure that we perfect the dark art of diatribe, so do we unfit ourselves for Christian encounters by which we learn and grow.

Group discussions will have to be characterized by a palpable trust in one another if they are to be availing. That blessed counselling of superiors and servicing of one another that group discussions should provide is a means of enlightenment. But we must expect that light is always going to give off a little heat. And the brighter the light, the more heat is generated. This is nothing to fear or even to suspect. It is only when a discussion gets acrid or scorching that we know we have a defective lighting system, or maybe have blown a spiritual fuse. A bit of heat and even a puff or two of generative smoke is perfectly normal.

The story is told of the Italian opera company at rehearsal. The baritone insisted that the soprano oversang in their duet; the soprano said the baritone couldn't read. The tenor flew into a fit of impatience over the endless repetitions of the duet. The director flung out both arms and pleaded with the soprano. "Pee-ahneeeeeeesimo, pleeeeeese!" his dark brow wrinkled with anguish and his Italian eyes full of the facile tears of the stricken Latin. The soprano stomped her foot. The baritone turned his back. The tenor paced the stage. But after the prescribed measure of tears had been filled up by the director, it all came right somehow. At any rate, the few bewildered and alarmed spectators who had been admitted to the rehearsal survived to watch the performers and the director conclude the stormy evening by falling upon one another's necks and departing in high spirits for an ample spaghetti dinner.

The most interesting thing about this story is that it is true. Let superiors and discussants expound its parable, each to himself.

IV   *Tactics for Revolution*

In its Decree on the Adaptation and Renewal of Religious Life, Vatican II was at some pains to underscore that freedom of choice about which so much is being presently said and written. It was a large, fresh concept that the Council Fathers underlined, not a pretty sloughing off of obligations or even of accepted wholesome conventions. Society does not generally applaud the nudist for having gotten free of his clothes. Nor do we ordinarily have a jamboree at the funeral of the man who proved himself too free to be bound by traffic laws. Most persons do not even give a standing ovation to the matron who appears at the Metropolitan in shorts and a pullover. Rather, we recognize these individuals as, among other things, quite limited in their concept of freedom. They are persons unable to respond to the calls of their own social milieu with intelligence and judgment.

Perfectae Caritatis points out that "members of each [religious] institute should recall first of all that by professing the evangelical counsels they responded to a divine call, so that by being not only dead to sin (cf. Rom 6:11) but also renouncing the world, they may live for God alone. They have dedicated their entire lives to His service" (no. 5). It is a neat exposition of the freedom of the soul called by God to the religious state. The person is called, not drafted. If he does not wish to respond, he need not go into hiding, make a public demonstration of burning the invitation, or even excuse himself. God says, "Come." The free person chooses to come or not to come. And this response will be the first of innumerable responses to be made in religious life, which is precisely a series of invitations and responses until the last shadow lengthens.

We are beginning to wriggle free of the dubious assumption that a vocation is a command from God and that, therefore, one called to the religious life will be lost outside it. It is rather, let us repeat it, an invitation that God proffers. He is not actively recruiting, but suggesting. It belongs to the person to accept or reject this invitation. Whether it would be possible to refuse such an invitation with impunity of conscience or whether the rejector could expect the fullness of peace that belongs to response freely given is matter for personal pondering and examination.

It would scarcely imply the presence of good manners, much less of good sense, to refuse a special invitation to dine with royalty, nor would a poor man likely be able to reproduce their menu. But he is free to accept, and not subject to penal law if he refuses. Actually, the men in the Gospel story who were too busy to attend the king's supper must have had some grave afterthoughts. Trying out oxen is calculated to whip up the appetite. Touring one's farmlands, the same. And even if the new bride of the third man was a good cook, it is doubtful whether she had the means or the skill to produce a royal banquet. The king did not say that the farmlands would waste, the oxen break their legs, or the wife prove a shrew. He simply said that those men would not taste of his supper. He apparently thought that was something worth pondering.

Young people today are hearing God's "Come!" They have a choice to make. For it is "Come!" God says, not "Get in there!" Perhaps in greater numbers than ever before, religious of our era are hearing God's repeated "Come!" against a counterchorus from the world, "Come out!" Again, there is a free choice to make. Vatican II only reminds such religious in gentle terms that they have responded to a *divine* call, have promised to die to sin and renounce the world. Significantly, the Decree adds, "They have dedicated their entire lives to His service. This constitutes a special consecration" (PC, no. 5).

Now, consecration of one's entire life to a particular service will obviously entail a continued giving of self. When that service is pledged directly to God, it must imply a full pouring out of one's self on the One served. Finity can never be adequate for the Infinite, but the very least it can give Infinity is the whole of its finity. Again, it reduces to spiritual good manners and good sense. Holiness is actually an expression of good manners toward God, just as it is the fullness of good sense.

Having, then, responded to a divine call, having renounced the world in order to give oneself utterly to God's service, it would scarcely indicate good manners or good sense to indulge in logical misfeats until we emerged with the strange conclusions that service of God is rendered by keeping a close eye on my own interests, that giving is better translated as "getting". It is true that personal fulfillment is a necessity for sound psychological functioning. But we are evolving some strange conceptions of personal fulfillment. If our occupation is a continual giving of ourselves to God and souls, we shall be utterly fulfilled without having to give this matter a single thought.

The outstanding heresy parasitical to renewal in religious life may well be that which unseats personal fulfillment as an effect of self-donation and inserts it as a cause for self-aggrandizement. To be acquisitive of love, of friendship, of learning, of skill, or of whatever for my personal fulfillment is to make religious life an affair of getting. But this is only the crude and obvious form of the heresy. More subtle is giving for the sake of getting. Put plainly, it is to be dedicated, committed, involved, energetic, outgoing just so that I may breathe in a sense of fulfillment. It is what T. S. Eliot has called "the highest treason: / To do the right deed for the wrong reason".[1]

Self-donation must be made without any thought of personal fulfillment if it is to be sincere. Paradoxically,

---

[1] *Murder in the Cathedral* (New York: Harcourt, Brace and Company, 1935), p. 44.

self-donation must disengage itself of any notion of personal fulfillment if it is to produce personal fulfillment.

It is a beautiful piece of *sequitur*, then, that the Decree proceeds in number 5 to speak of the emptying out of oneself, and this as a sharing in Christ's emptying of himself (cf. Phil 2:7). The document does not leave us musing for ways to unclutter ourselves. It comes forward with swift specifics and calls attention to the fact that a real service of God ought to inspire and feed the virtues particularly conducive to that emptying out of self which is essential to real service. It mentions four virtues enjoying no great popularity in the world: humility, obedience, fortitude, and chastity. Franciscans can continue their search for a "return to the original spirit of [their] institutes" (PC, no. 2) and keep their founder's "spirit and special aims ... set before them" (PC, no. 2b) by examining these unpopular virtues in popular Francis, their father.

As has already been noted, one of Saint Francis' outstanding qualities as superior was his humble willingness to listen to others and his humble readiness to admit a mistake and rectify it. *Il Poverello*, the dear little poor one—how the title becomes him! We find that "little" recurring almost incessantly in his biographies yet without a suggestion of the precious or the saccharine. He knew himself to be and showed himself to be a little man with a great work to do.

Often he was thwarted and frustrated, as is anyone who ever undertakes a work of value or tries to achieve a worthwhile end. Sometimes he felt ready to abandon his whole enterprise when the waves of opposition, of cunning and connivery, of treachery and betrayal threatened to engulf him. Nowhere does Francis reveal himself more appealingly human and vulnerable than when he tells Brother Leo he will go off and live in a cave by himself and "let them do what they want." Yet that fortitude which *Perfectae Caritatis* links with humility as among the virtues that a real service of God should inspire reasserted itself in Francis after that understandable and endearing slackening of spirit. His humility was fed by his fortitude; his fortitude drew its strength from his humility. Francis was not a "blamer". When he made mistakes, he had the fortitude and the humility to acknowledge them. When others made mistakes, he had the fortitude and the humility not to editorialize on them. Do not we sometimes show a rather striking deficiency in such acknowledgments and a rather outstanding talent for such editorializing?

With the upsurge of enthusiasm for the renewal of religious life comes inevitably a great deal of spray. Our human hazard lies in the tendency to give up pursuing the renewal for the excitement of watching the spray. Enthusiasm and excitement are not the same things. Most persons must be convinced by now that our times are changing as times have had a way of doing since time began, that religious are called to meet the challenge as Vatican II has urged, that vegetation is not an apostolate in the modern Church nor hibernation correct methodology. We do not need to go on editorializing on the fact, as though our needle had gotten stuck.

Most religious are happily realizing that we have often not been athletes with Saint Paul nor run in his race. We have lagged behind Christ and his ever-fresh challenge. We have not actualized our potential in the Church. It is so good to feel this way. The great tragedy would be to feel that we have been doing rather well, really; what in the world would we find to improve on? But we need to be *calm* even in acknowledging our own failures, and much more in pointing out those of others. Failure to keep pace with God's challenges, to be true Christians, is not a spiritual plague endemic to our age. Quite some time has passed since God said of his people, "Stiff-necked and hard of heart! How long shall I bear with you?" Before Christianity, people were surprisingly like people today. They found it difficult to take God at his word. They were sometimes lazy, often indifferent. And even in the midst of manna spread like the hoarfrost about them, they preferred cucumbers and garlic. So, too, did Jesus have his patience tried: "O perverse and hardhearted generation!" And, "How long shall I put up with you?" Even at the Ascension, his elect band, the apostles, were still hopefully inquiring whether the earthly millennium of which they had stubbornly continued to dream through forty days with a risen God was not about to dawn.

There is at present a beautiful revolution blessedly raging in the Church. A real revolution, that is, a returning. A revolving of the spiritual wheel that may have run down a bit, even quite a bit. Francis our father incited a tremendous spiritual and social revolution in his own age, but our revolutionist had too much to do with only one lifetime to do it in, to spend his energies inveighing against those who had failed to oil the spiritual wheel in the past.

Saint Francis need not have looked very far afield to dis-cover any number of clerics and seculars who had defi-nitely not been doing the right thing. There were many abuses in the hierarchical structure of the Church of his time. Avaricious prelates, venal clergy, cantankerous and comfort-loving nuns were not at all unknown in his era. Yet, Fran-cis never raged against them. He simply was poor, was chaste, was loving and gentle. He was the genuine revolu-tionary. He got things going, set wheels revolving by the only force that ever generates enduring action: love.

It is simply a fact that we can have too many workshops and discussions on such subjects as the formation of nov-ices and juniors, the psychological aspects of religious life, and mental hygiene, which reduce to mere long-ringing condemnations of the past. One, of course, would be too many. We could be using this time and this energy actu-ally forming our communities, in studying and promot-ing a sound psychology of religious life, and in practicing and encouraging mental hygiene. We are all surely aware that mistakes have been made in the past. We may even be willing to admit that we have made a few ourselves. Let us go on from there, not hold a seminar there. Let us by all means get expert guidance in the areas just mentioned and many others, the while not letting the fact elude us that the Holy Spirit remains *the* Expert, *the* Counsellor. There may certainly be valid reasons for calmly mentioning some past errors for mutual education. A charitable sharing of blunders can be a genuine service to one another, since we all stumble often enough even when forewarned of booby traps. However, to talk from a stump of censure will never avail anything positive.

Francis Cardinal Spellman of New York once had a splendid sentence on this point in an address. After remarking that "whenever a revolution occurs, there are always some who consider it an invitation to change nearly everything; to challenge too much; to destroy what is vital and necessary along with that which has outlived its time", he adds, "This is change for the sake of change, and while the voices which clamor for it are a small minority, they are loud and they disturb the peace of the revolution." [2]

The peace of the revolution. It is preserved by the humility and the fortitude of the revolutionists, and in equal proportions. In their perfection, these virtues particularly urged in *Perfectae Caritatis*, number 5, blend into each other. Only a courageous man is strong enough to be humble. Only a truly humble man is conditioned for bravery. For the proud man, there is only bravado.

Saint Francis had the courage to swim against the tide in his own age, and his strokes were so sure and strong because they were made by a humble man. He blessed the world with an entirely new concept of religious life, yet he never once ranted against old concepts. He never blamed anyone for not joining his revolution. He was too busy waging it. That may even be part of the explanation of how he could be patient with those most difficult of all persons to endure: the apathetic.

Privileged to live in this marvelous era of challenge and change, we shall want to take care not to disturb the peace of the revolution. "*Pax et bonum!*" remains the greatest of revolutionary cries.

[2] Quoted in *The North Country Catholic*, vol. 54, no. 66 (August 14, 1966).

And then, obedience and chastity are held before us in number 5 of *Perfectae Caritatis* as the virtues that a real service of God should also inspire. Certainly they shone in Saint Francis and Saint Clare. They both had an obedience crisis beyond what any of us can ever suffer simply because it involved not a person but an Order. Both had loving and well-intentioned superiors (namely, popes) who couldn't see it their way. It was not a field of apostolate, an assignment, a treasured project that was threatened. It was their very life—their Rule.

It was only on her deathbed that Clare was given ecclesiastical approbation for a Rule she knew was from God and of God. Francis had not even that late consolation in the same dramatic measure. But because theirs was "a *real* service of God", obedience was their special art. These two proficient artists had cracked the code of the supernatural and understood that it is the utter surrender of the roots of one's desires and one's very being to God that alone avails for full Christian renewal. This kind of obedience is at once the highest form of poverty. Its effects are a deepening of chastity.

The celibate should normally be the most loving, warmhearted, and compassionate of persons. Coldness of manner, indifference to the needs of others, self-centeredness, remoteness—all these indicate a malfunctioning of consecrated virginity. But we shall want to dwell on this later.

We are presently somewhat preoccupied with personality and the development of natural gifts. It might be better merely to be occupied. For it is good and proper to insist that grace builds on nature, but it is important that we clarify what it is in nature that grace builds on. We have this holy paradox in religious life, that we must develop each his own nature and yet be at enmity with nature. The key to the paradox lies in the very simplest of expressions: a supernatural life. It is to this that we are called, to a life not stifling or destroying nature, but definitely above nature.

While we are most justifiably concerned that religious life should not be unnatural, we may need to remind ourselves that it has to be supernatural. Nature is the material with which we work out our salvation and our religious perfection, yet nature has this propensity for beckoning us down the wrong road. Original sin has bequeathed to human nature the perverse talent for taking the wrong direction, and the old and simple truth goes on emerging each new century: nature let go its own way goes down. "He who strives for the mastery refrains himself from all things" (1 Cor 9:25). Humility and fortitude, obedience and chastity, are prescribed by *Perfectae Caritatis* for effecting that emptying out of self which alone fits us to be co-workers with Christ. The development of individual gifts and talents does not require a divorce from supervision, but a deeper wedded life with it. The blossoming of one's personality is not a possibility only of the fraternal authority set-up. That is, in fact, where it least flourishes. To say everything one thinks, to do everything one likes, to decide all things for oneself is to bring forth green leaves likely enough—like poison ivy.

Perfectae Caritatis has not hesitated to sing an unpopular tune: the emptying out of oneself as Christ emptied himself. It is possible to be so eager to do something for God and for souls as to forget that what God needs for new witness to his love is not people who can do something but people through whom he can do something—uncluttered people who have emptied themselves out with Christ in his humanity.

There was once a brave and humble little man who declared he would obey a novice of one day if that lad were superior, and whose virginal love was so identified with the love of Christ for mankind that it broke out in the sacred stigmata. He spread joy like an epidemic, though probably few men have suffered more. And he never disturbed the peace of the revolutionary renewal that God had inspired him to incite, because he was so busy emptying himself of Francis so that Christ could live in him, that he never had time or taste for declaiming against anyone else.

This is not to defend superiors who have made mistakes in the past and may be making them now. It is not even to defend those under them, who may perhaps make a few errors also. Least of all is it to defend an indefensible status quo. It is only to say that even while Saint Francis burned with enthusiasm for his tremendous God-given dream, he still knew how to suffer and to wait. It is only to suggest that one reason Saint Francis was able to press forward so quickly was that he never wasted time on disdainful looks backward.

V *An Outstanding Gift of Grace*

That chastity is not something that claps padlocks on the heart is made very clear in the first number devoted to this subject in *Perfectae Caritatis*. For too long and in too many quarters the chastity proper to the religious state has been approached from a negative viewpoint. It has frequently been presented and accepted more as a giving up than as a giving. Number 12 of *Perfectae Caritatis* reminds us that it is not only definitely a giving, but that it is first a gift from God to us before it is a gift from us to God.

"An outstanding gift of grace" is Vatican II's description of the chastity that religious profess (PC, no. 12). In this compact expression is the answer to those who are not so much a part of that social contingent sincerely concerned over the question of celibacy as of a mob

47

agitation over an overpopularized problem. Actually, celibacy itself is not a "problem", although it is certainly
true that perseverance in celibacy may present problems—
and even acute problems—to the individual celibate. This
is merely one instance of the manipulation of terms at
which certain modern writers are so adept. Even without any literary exposé of the spurious logic endemic to
such writing, we might harbor some fleeting doubts about
the *sans réproche* crusading spirit of the supposedly tor-
tured ex-priest for his fellow sufferers when he invites
the reporters and cameramen to catch him with his gui-
tar before the new crib in the living room. A genuine
agony of conscience does not commonly request that cam-
eras be set up.

When the "outstanding gift of grace" that is religious
chastity has not been given by God, there are certainly
going to be multiple problems for the one who professes
celibacy. There may well be problems also for the celibate
who has received this gift of grace, but to say this is to
be far indeed from saying that celibacy itself is a problem. "He that can take it, let him take it", was our Savior's
terse conclusion in this matter. To whom the outstanding gift of grace is given, let them respond with the gift
of an undivided heart. For such, celibacy is not a problem but "the most suitable means" (PC, no. 12) of dedication to God and his Church.

For anything, however, that requires a surrender of
something so radical to human nature as the instinct to
give oneself to a human spouse and fulfill the beautiful
need to bring forth new life, a force beyond and above
nature will be needed. One of the most important duties

of superiors in screening applicants to the religious life and in evaluating them within the context of community life in the formation period will be to try to discover whether this force is present, whether this "outstanding gift of grace" has been given to this person. Its presence will happily betray itself in many ways. Its absence can, at least in many cases, be noted in behavioral patterns we want to consider here.

Most young people entering religious life today have inescapably been exposed to the sensation-barrage of modern living. They know more about "life" than those who have preceded them into religion by twenty or perhaps even ten years. "Life" is served up to them on drugstore bookracks whose wares, even though unsampled, retain their powers of visual assault. It is thrown at them from billboards and projected on video, television, and movie screens. "Life" is droned at them in dentists' waiting rooms by radioed sopranos who can at least be commended for their valor in singing when apparently afflicted with acute sinusitis. Yet, these same prematurely wise young people often know nothing-minus about that form of life which is most pertinent to them: their own. It is imperative that they be educated in the science of human behavior and particularly, in the case of young women, of typical feminine responses to persons, situations, and circumstances.

Experience indicates, for example, that it is vital in the formation period of a young religious woman that she be helped to understand the recurring emotional cycles that are concurrent with physical cycles, and to deal with them as a responsible adult. Such instruction could cast out the

bewilderment, the fears, and the discouragement that often
plague novices and junior sisters, stunting their spiritual
growth and hindering that full flowering of love which
should characterize the virginally consecrated religious. As
Perfectae Caritatis points out, the chastity proper to the religious life is not meant to constrict the heart but to free "the
heart of man in a unique fashion so that it may be more
inflamed with love for God and for all men" (no. 12).

A woman with stunted powers of loving is among the
most pitiable of all creatures. For love is really the meaning of woman. It is her supreme motivation and itself
her apostolate. And it always calls for expression in surrender. As the married woman has the privilege to surrender herself to another person in a very special fashion,
so does the religious woman enjoy the privilege of surrendering her heart's whole affection to God in the unique
manner of the vow of chastity. We do not vow chastity
to something but to Someone. The religious woman deliv-
ers her entire power and expression of loving back to the
God who gave them to her. It is sound theology that
suggests a wedding ring for her finger as sign of such a
giving, one taught by the credibly good theologians who
have stated clearly in *Perfectae Caritatis* that "in this way
[by the vow of chastity] they recall to the minds of all
the faithful that wondrous marriage decreed by God and
which is to be fully revealed in the future age in which
the Church takes Christ as its only spouse" (no. 12). It
indicates a sturdy practical-mindedness that some wear a
ring as part of this recalling.

A woman can give her time and her energy to a
cause. She can give herself only to a person. The bridal

relationship of each soul to God, the feminine aspect of the whole people of God before his gaze in all salvation history, is strikingly imaged in the virginally consecrated religious woman. Some testimony to that bridal relationship of the Church with Christ to which the religious woman bears striking witness should be rendered in every profession ceremony. It must be made clear that a woman entering into the full community life of an Order is not joining an organization but surrendering herself to God in the context of her religious family that she may be utterly committed to his Church. It is significant that *Perfectae Caritatis* couples in a single sentence the giving of oneself to God and to the works of one's religious apostolate and sets down religious chastity as the most suitable means for doing both.

It is also not without significance that the Council Fathers showed themselves less naïve than many an avant-garde in this matter of religious chastity. They were practical-minded men who did not believe that precaution is nonrelevant to a technological age. After that lyric passage about the wondrous marriage in which the Church takes Christ as her spouse, these draftsmen of *Perfectae Caritatis* turn with the ease of theologians whose feet are as firmly on earth as their heads are above the clouds, to some no-nonsense counselling. Religious who are striving faithfully to observe the chastity they have professed, the Fathers remind us, should not overestimate their own strength but practice mortification and custody of the senses. And that such homely, old-fashioned practices as self-abnegation and discipline of the senses are conducive to clear thinking is urged by them when they immediately go on to say, "As a result they will not be influenced by those false doctrines which scorn perfect continence as being impossible or harmful to human development and they will repudiate by a certain spiritual instinct everything which endangers chastity" (PC, no. 12). Maybe we need to ponder the converse of that. It would read as follows: "If religious striving to observe chastity overestimate their own strength and do not practice mortification or custody of the senses, they will be highly vulnerable to and influenced by those false doctrines which scorn perfect continence as being impossible or harmful to human development. Neither will they repudiate by a certain spiritual instinct everything which endangers chastity, for they will have blunted that instinct by disuse."

Religious are asked by Vatican II not to "neglect the natural means which promote health of mind and body", and superiors especially are urged to "remember that chastity is guarded more securely when true brotherly love flourishes in the common life of the community." If this is true for all religious, it wants to be underscored for religious women. If expressed sisterly love has been sometimes tolerated, sometimes suspected, it has definitely not everywhere flourished. To flourish, to flower—is it not to put out petals that can be seen, appreciated, enjoyed? Sisterly love as a nebulous concept has always been highly acceptable, of course. As something both warmly atmospheric and practically expressed, however, it has not always been so enthusiastically welcomed. To be so occupied with brooming "particular" friendships out of the community as to create a prophylactic atmosphere in the convent would certainly not be to show forth the spirit of Saint Francis and Saint Clare. They would have none of this.

We recall how the seraphic father's particularly loved son, Brother Juniper, found the earth quite barren when his special friend Brother Amazialbene left it. That he testified to the tenderness of his affection for his departed friend by expressing the desire to make himself a soup plate and cup out of the two halves of Amazialbene's skull, which he longed to divide for this purpose, may not exactly set our lips quivering with sympathy for the plan, but Juniper foresaw the limitations of more conventional men. "They would not understand", he remarked sadly. So Amazialbene's skull remained in place on his skeleton, but Juniper continued to bewail the separation from his great friend.

Saint Clare encouraged true friendship to the extent of making it a point of her Rule. "And if a mother loves and nurtures her physical daughter, how much more lovingly ought a sister love and nurture her spiritual sister!" We do not nurture one another with clichés but with compassion and affection.

True, it is important to remember that affection in religious life has a different expression than affection outside religious life. It obviously cannot be a matter of endearments or caresses, nor may it be a spiritual intrusion. But it is just as warm and human and vital, and even more so because it is ennobled by that unaffected dignity and sweet reserve which we expect virginal consecration to produce, and rooted in a common self-donation to Christ.

If chastity is more securely guarded in an atmosphere of flourishing love, we may go forward from that point and maintain that chastity itself flourishes in such an environment. For chastity, as remarked above, is not just something to be guarded, not material for padlocks. It is, in fact, much more related to a greenhouse than to a safety-deposit vault. Love, like goodness, is diffusive of itself. It seeks its own expression. What we need to do is to encourage its appropriate expressions in religious life, not to abort them.

That sisters be interested in one another's families; aware of family illnesses, employment problems, and the like; and concerned about these things to the extent that they express the concern can be one among hundreds of manifestations of normal affection in community life. There are occasions for giving spontaneous assistance to a sister who looks unusually tired. There are ways of exhibiting compassion, sympathy, and appreciation that in no measure disrupt silence, not even that more comprehensive silence proper to a cloister, but rather charge silence with warmth and vitality. Women have always been ingenious at devising means to express their love. Religious women should perfect this native expertness, not blunt it. There is also the art of praise that can play so important a part in healthy psychological living in the convent. However intent we are on doing things for God alone, we react positively to the expressed appreciation of others if we are normal. It is well to remember that other normal persons react in this same way to our sincere praise and appreciation. It is important in a community that each sister makes the others aware that she knows they are alive, that she is interested in them and affected by them.

A woman's talent for seeing everything can be directed down one of two paths in religious life. Either she can spotlight every defect in her companions or she can train her batteries on the good in her sisters, which sometimes needs and even desperately needs just such highlighting to establish itself as radical in the development of "person". The trouble about spotlighting defects in others, of course, is that it throws into obscurity the lighter's own defects. At that point and according to the degree of the obscurity, her own development as a spiritual person ceases.

The false idea of divorcing similar interests also needs to be hauled before the tribunal of renewal. Why should not sisters with human interests, natural talents, cultural tastes in common be allowed on suitable occasions to share these? At one Poor Clares' Institute in religious formation and related areas, a number of the abbesses and mistresses stressed this point. While the danger of chipping up community recreation into hobby groups to the detriment of full familial involvement is a real one, it is not really formidable if a community is functioning with easy love and not chugging with frustration and strain. There are occasions of extra recreation when such sharings could easily be made without detriment to the full-circle joy of the ordinary community recreation.

There is, as a matter of fact, danger in everything. There is danger in eating. You might choke on a fishbone. It is perilous to walk down the stairs. Lots of people have broken a hip that way. Part of the whole happy wave of what renewal should be may be the de-emphasizing of danger and an underlining of positive factors. There will always be extremists and immature faddists who disclaim the existence of danger. Against these, Vatican II warns us, and specifically in number 12 of *Perfectae Caritatis*. However, it is quite possible to be aware of hazards and take precautions against them without being paralyzed in the face of hazards. Thus, encouraging a sharing of common interests among religious in a community may lead to exclusivism. But the point to work on will not be the sharing of interests but the religious who are too immature to share and so can only devour. The fault will not lie with the opportunity but with persons not yet equipped to use it properly.

Given a community atmosphere where warm human affection, reinforced by and rooted in a true spiritual ideal, flourishes, young religious preparing to make a vow of chastity and older ones already dedicated to God and Church in this singular way should be testifying to the community their growth in love. How? Perhaps primarily by an increasing necessity to give, give of their energy, their interest, their affection, their sympathy. The urge to surrender herself and to spend herself, which is basic to woman and which is exercised in marriage and family life in a special manner, will also be apparent in the virginally consecrated religious woman if her vow of chastity is really operative in her and will find increasing ways to exercise itself in healthy community life.

Conjugal love is only one expression of love. Sisterly love and spiritually maternal love for souls are expressions just as valid. Sacrifice and self-donation are characteristic of all genuine love. If they do not appear and develop in a religious, then there is something malfunctioning in either her concept of religious chastity, her training in religious life, or perhaps the structures of her community life, which in some cases could militate against such manifestation and development. "They should be so instructed as to be able to undertake the celibacy which binds them to God in a way which will benefit their entire personality" (PC, no. 12).

If a religious is steadily growing in compassion, if she has a zest for her duties and exhibits real generosity, if the vitality of her interests is apparent, and if she is increasingly better able to handle herself, her emotions, and her moods, we can take all these manifestations of maturity as signs of an operative vow of chastity also. On the other hand, either a severity toward others or a clinging attachment to others, apathy for duties and halfheartedness in community enterprises, general lethargy, and a diminishing ability to take herself and her moods in hand and establish better emotional balance could well be signs that religious chastity is either not understood or has not been taught. It might even be a sign that God's "outstanding gift of grace" is not present.

Perfectae Caritatis, number 12, urges that candidates for the vow of chastity must show themselves "to possess the required psychological and emotional maturity" to make it. While this certainly does not mean that only psychologically and emotionally finished human products are eligible to make the vow, it does direct us to look for development. It need not be cause for alarm that young religious act immaturely and often let their emotions gallop away with them. If, however, these young religious are not gradually growing in the realization of their immaturity, it may be time to question their suitability for a celibate life. They may not always be able to apply the reins on the unbroken horses riding their emotional range, but they should be able to recognize that reins are indicated. This is part of that undivided giving to God which is intrinsic to religious chastity. Such an undivided giving to him will inevitably flow back upon the giver, sanctified by him for sharing with others.

It is only love that really releases all the potential of a human heart, a human being. Thus it is important that religious women be educated in the vow of chastity, which is their expression of love both to God and to souls. And they have a right to expect in religious life the kind of atmosphere conducive to their development as persons. Given God's gift, proper instruction, and appropriate context, it will be each individual's choice as to how vital a womanly force she will be in the life of her community and thus in the life of the Church.

VI   ... And Possessing All Things

In the very real poverty of the beginning years of our Roswell foundation, we were blessed with the gift (immense to us) of an open-reel tape recorder. As we would occasionally listen to tape recordings, we reflected on our advantage over those who had only depersonalized tape recorders. Ours was highly personalized, by which is meant that unless a living person turned the reels, they would not revolve with any predictable dependability. The ancient recorder, today a relic in the convenience-oriented world of recording technology, served the community with laudable devotedness. It brought us the voices of our sisters in other monasteries at home and abroad, ushered the outstanding theologians of our age into our cloister, gave us bonus retreats, and played in our refectory return engagements of Blackfriars' production of our plays. The day finally came, however, when we had to admit that its old mechanical heart simply wasn't what it used to be.

After a dozen valiant turns, it would shudder from the effort and stop to rest. And the machine's frequent salubrious pauses tended to produce such very odd auditory effects that we found it necessary to call in an engineer. That is, one of the nuns, perched on a high stool next to the tape recorder in the middle of the refectory during our evening repast, would insert her right index finger into the left reel's chest cavity and stimulate the heart action. These constant manual revolutions would rouse Seraphim (the name given to our tape recorder in salvation history) to new efforts. Each evening at the beginning of collation, I would announce the names of the sisters who were to take ten-minute turns at this engineering feat, and thoughts inevitably arose in my heart as I did so. One was satisfaction that no one ever laughed. Even today, it does not seem in any way ludicrous for a Poor Clare tape recorder to function only with sisterly aid. Another was the happy contentment of knowing that the gift of a new tape recorder, should God provide it (and he did indeed do so eventually), would fulfill a real need, and not be a mere convenience to clutter our life. A third was a serene joy that both these things were true.

It seems safe to say that most religious have sincerely sought for a new and realistic witness to the voluntary poverty that *Perfectae Caritatis* says in number 13 is "highly esteemed especially today as an expression of the following of Christ." Anyone who has had the opportunity to speak personally to many young religious in this generation will have discovered the holy unrest among them as they reach out for sincere and timely expressions of poverty. Sometimes they sound critical. They question. They summon the community before the tribunal of their desperate need to find us genuine. Actually, they are not usually critical so much as simply seeking to be part of the constructiveness and the resurgence that are churning within the very heart of Holy Church herself in these wonderfully challenging times. It is our business either to bring believable answers to their questions or honestly to admit that we do not know the answers and initiate a community search party to look for them. It is our duty to be found genuine.

There are few things more disconcerting in the present preoccupation with evangelical poverty, however, than the spectacle of religious who are ardent and glib in the panel discussions, but surprisingly weighted down in their own lives. It is certainly not hypocrisy. It appears to be lack of integration of life and a want of coordination in living.

Perfectae Caritatis allowed for new forms of voluntary poverty. As they were sought and experimented with by communities and Orders, it became clear that it is more important than is realized in some quarters to seek an individual renovation as well. The most availing way to share the poverty and insecurity of the inner-city dwellers remains basically to live poorly and insecurely when one is not physically in the inner city. It is no good to emerge from a maze of comforts and the small clutter of conveniences to serve the poor and then return to the maze and the clutter. The best gift a religious can bring the poor is her own poverty. The highest service we can render the world's deprived is the joy-bringing of our voluntary deprivation.

Obviously, this does not mean or even imply that religious must live in destitution if they are to have fellowship with the destitute. Still less does it suggest that compassion for squalor can spring only from unloveliness of life in one's own surroundings. Rather, whether seemingly or actually paradoxical, it is most often just the opposite. "Involvement" and "relevancy" are the darling words of the hour. We want to be on guard against the threat that popular phrases invariably pose: superficiality.

Both involvement and relevancy belong primarily to the spirit, to the heart that expresses them exteriorly. Thus, there is for religious only one authentic involvement with the poor, and that is to be poor. Without an interior attitude of poorness, one can have no proper fellowship with the poor. More especially, one cannot be a cleansing agent in the swelter and sweat of unbeautiful poverty unless one is oneself clean and uncluttered of heart. Lacking freedom ourselves, we cannot be a liberator to those whom misery fetters. We can only teach them the worse and deeper misery that is servitude to conveniences or ease.

It is the quality of our being that touches and ennobles the poor beyond any service we can perform for them and even beyond any external sharing of lots. That is why it is equally possible for the cloistered nun or the priest to serve the poor. It is merely a case of different external expressions of the same quality of being.

If we study the poverty of our seraphic Father Francis, we quickly discover several of its striking characteristics.

Two of these were his decreasing material needs and his increasing capacity for enjoyment. The poorer Francis became, the less cramped was his soul. Because he had such a zest for eliminating unessentials, his talent for enjoying life's good things grew steadily more highly sensitized. There must be very few men who ever had less of earth's goods than Saint Francis had after his conversion. But there has probably never been a man who had such a good time on earth despite the plenitude of his sufferings. Even more particularly, there is likely no one who enjoyed the good things of earth more. Because he was so clean and uncluttered of heart, Francis had eyes to see the pleasurable things that busier men have no time to see, and he drained the pleasure out of them with an enthusiasm that sometimes annoyed and sometimes disconcerted those of his brethren who were lesser friars in a sense not intended by the saint when he named his brotherhood.

Brother Masseo found it irritating that hungry Saint Francis could feel so festal over odd bits of bread and a running stream. He could not even summon up any particular admiration for the furniture. While Francis thrilled to the graciousness of God, who had provided a table just beside the water supply, poor Masseo could not see anything but a flat stone. Furthermore, thought Masseo, the stone had always been there. It was just one more of those "anyhow" things of life, not worth his attention. And so the two friars picnicked together, but only one had a thoroughly good time. It is probably safe to say that Saint Francis would also have enjoyed wine instead of water, almond cakes instead of bread. But the important thing was that he could enjoy either one. The point is Francis' talent for having a good time. For it is the talent of the truly poor who have elected to be so for the love of the poor Christ.

The *Poverello* might have considerable trouble of mind over our clichés about giving up pleasure that we may have joy. His own life makes it quite clear that Francis, who certainly held the secret of joy, by no means despised pleasure. He found pleasure in song and embarrassed Brother Elias by calling for singing as death came upon him. It shook some people to witness a man having a good time dying, which is just what Francis did, as Saint Clare did after him, thanking God on her deathbed for his thoughtfulness to have created her.

Few things could be more ludicrous than depicting Saint Francis as a gourmet, just as few things could be more disgusting than claiming he was a gourmand. But we may miss the vital principle if we simply laugh or are merely repelled. Francis was not a gourmand at life's broad table of pleasures because he respected and appreciated good things too much to devour them in such quantity as to lose the power to savor them. He was not a gourmet among the delights of living because he was never that tired or that bored with simplicity. The robe of his freedom was too beautiful to be spoiled with ruffles.

Now, is this way of thinking mere idealistic spinning of words? Is it not even foolishness to talk of beauty and pleasure and freedom to the wretchedly poor who live in squalor and misery and embittered dependence? Probably it is. Likely enough it would be the worst thing we could possibly do. However, to talk and to be are definitely not the same thing. Each can exist (and often enough do) independently of the other. So we could venture to say that as unavailing as it is to talk of beauty and pleasure and freedom to those who do not have them and who may be too involved with hunger and cold and insecurity even to aspire toward anything but the immediate assuagement of those needs, just so availing is it that we should bring to the poor and suffering the quality of our poor being, our own voluntary poverty that must be beautiful, joyous, and free if it is authentic.

There is a deep relationship between the present search for valid and currently meaningful expressions of evangelical poverty and the present enthusiam for healthier concepts of mortification than have prevailed in some areas of religious life in past centuries. That searchers can get off the track and enthusiasts get carried away to a new extreme is only to be expected if we have understood anything at all of the pattern of human history over a test period of some two thousand years or managed to pick up a few bits of presently relevant information from the behavioral graphs of our pre-Christianity forebears. If it is not surprising, however, it is certainly something indicating action to be taken, action as elementary as getting back on the track and as radical as establishing balance. Thus we shall not want to testify to our awareness of the need for a presently convincing witness of poverty by fulminations against past and perhaps cozier concepts of it. This was never Saint Francis' way, as has already been mentioned.

We shall simply want ourselves to search and, with God's help and our blessed Father Francis' inspiration, hope to find. Neither would we manifest an especially striking

grasp of mortification by shouting down the mortifica-
tions others have practiced in the past, still less by descend-
ing to contempt of them. We shall want only to recover
a vision that does seem to have gotten, if not lost, at
least obscured somewhere down the path of the centuries since the earth was fortunate enough to have Saint
Francis walking around on it.

The poor and mortified man is the freely dying man.
He has chosen to be without many things so that he
may more easily be God's, for he knows that overdoses
of earth have the same power of enslaving the addict as
doses of any other drug. He has discovered the pearly
paradox of losing one's life to find it and being killed
with the psalmist all the day long—but for a reason. It is
invariably only the dying man who appreciates to the
full the beauty and joy of life. This seems to be the healthy
and invigorating idea that is struggling to extricate itself
from the "new look" in mortification, or rather in the
lack of it, which is actually a painted clown's face over
the truly noble features beneath.

In the same way that really great Christian humorists
always take God very seriously, Saint Francis was joyous
in poverty, lighthearted in self-discipline, bent on losing
his life so that he might save it. He always took God at
his word, and so he thought that falling into the furrow
of earth's sorrows in order to bring forth much fruit not
at all an unattractive modus vivendi. We have presently
too many reenactments of the odd spectacle of seeds trying to climb up and out of the furrow. For isn't this what
we do when we pretend that mortification and self-
discipline are outmoded, that when our Lord threatened

that such seeds would "remain alone", he meant only pre-twenty-first-century seeds?

Saint Francis was a thoroughgoing realist. He did not extol the beauties of the primrose to beggars scarcely able to support the intolerable stench of their own leprous bodies. He first washed and fed the lepers and gave them his own exquisite courtesy, not as an alms but as their due. Then, because he was what he was, Francis made it possible for lepers to discover the primrose for themselves.

So, too, we can relieve the poor with alms, with service, with all manner of involvement, but we cannot heal the poor with anything except the quality of our own poverty. And of this they will be aware with the merciless acumen of longtime sufferers. Each religious will have to look to the quality of his own poverty if there is to be a communal renovation in this area, and doubtless many avenues for improvement will be opened in community discussions as well as in private examens. A few practical suggestions are offered here.

For some of us there may be a need to revise our ideas about asking for things. There is sometimes among religious a tendency to go along on the principle that anything that is given us rather than purchased is suitable for us to have. This can be a reasonably sure method for the development of the streamlined convent, the effete monastery, the house of studies-in-convenience. God forbid there should ever be a Franciscan house that has no inconveniences and offers every comfort. How will the spirit of Francis lodge in such a place? Yet sometimes, without a conscious volition, but by the Drift Method so successful in undermining communal poverty, we can come to pursue convenience as a kind of goal. This is immediately to have no part with the poor, whose lot is ever to be inconvenienced, to be made to wait, to live often on makeshifts. We are by no means execrating the ordinary conveniences of modern living for religious. It is not necessarily a triumph of poverty to squander time, either. Nor is inconvenience an ideal of itself. It is probably all right to use the conveniences and devices proper to middle-class families. We can know for sure whether it is by the way we react when deprived of conveniences. We can then find out whether they have become a goal.

We cannot produce an oversimplification, however. How hospitals and colleges can be maintained and administered in proper Franciscan style presents an overwhelmingly large field for exploration. The problems are multitudinous. And to drop them all into the lap of a lay administrator while we keep to the patient's bedside or at the student's side is as theoretically ideal a solution as it is assuredly fertile with new problems. Still, provocative thoughts do come of our trying to envision just how Saint Francis would run a hospital today or in what manner he would preside over a university, or, for that matter, an outlying mission. We want to be careful not to sigh away the suggestions that such speculations present to our minds with the regretful verdict that these are "idealistic, impractical". Sometimes the idealistic solution is surprisingly practical. However, it is always extremely demanding. It may demand, for one thing, more commitment than we had bargained for. It may suggest a witness possible only to the totally God-given religious.

That there is a direct ratio between charity and poverty in a community is as empirically undeniable as is the inverse ratio existing between materialities and joy in the community. Father Bernard Häring, C.Ss.R., has said much in his terse remark that when we have joy, we do not need many things. Probably most if not all superiors have experience of the reverse side of that statement also. It is the religious deficient in love and in joy who needs many, many things. There is seldom a more peevish individual than a religious who has everything.

We must be ever so careful not to become so enthusiastic about great new ventures for the community that we lose contact with the daily small realities. We need wholesome food, but not dainty or luxurious or even junk food. We have to get things done, but we cannot afford to forget that waiting is the particular art of the poor. We require an adequate dwelling, but adequacy is never pretentiousness. One of the most rewarding of life's hours is that in which we come to realize how very little we need. And here we have come full circle around to Saint Francis' capacity for enjoyment on which we began. Life turns sickening on the tongue when it is forever served up à la mode.

Another suggestion for the agenda of our renewal of poverty is for an examination of the "begging" principle. We can become glib about calling ourselves beggars and even point to the fruits of our begging with what seems pardonable pride in a good haul. But what does it mean to be a beggar? Is it not to be the utterly dependent one, the one who cannot have unless it be given him? The beggar who begs after the manner of the collector must be recognized as a collector and not as a beggar. One truly begs when one begs only for actual needs. It is not the office of the beggar to beg for conveniences. It is simply a matter of record that some of us have reduced "begging" to the level of soliciting things for which we have no real need at all.

"Let them confidently send for alms", writes Saint Clare in her Rule, but only after she has made it very plain how her daughters are to live. It is after they have worked hard and when they have discovered the regal joy of being "heiresses and queens of the kingdom of heaven" in the same measure that they are "pilgrims and strangers in this world" that they may humbly ask for such of their modest needs as they cannot supply of themselves. It is possible for religious to open a charge account on society. This is an area where superiors need to be less the master listeners than the plain talkers and the firm doers. If we want Saint Francis' joy, we must have his poverty. If we hope to enjoy life as he did, we must preserve his sense of wonder, the wonder that is poisoned by surfeit and ease.

Both of the foregoing suggestions might be made functional through this third: that each religious be helped to maintain contact with reality. Religious who never make a purchase, pay a bill, or see an account can gradually move into a never-never world as regards all material values. The solution is not to give each religious a salary, apartment, and bank account in order to be "in touch" with material realities; instead, there can be a fuller sharing of the community's financial concerns with all the professed members. While the superior is set to bear the actual burden of the materialities of the house, province, or order, and the religious ought to be left free of *all* the *details* of conventual commerce, there remains a very large area in which each religious can be very properly and efficaciously involved.

There is something else, though. It is the education of personal judgment. It cannot be denied that much of the criticism leveled against easy permissions these days is well deserved. The idea that a very perfect practice of poverty consists solely in having only what is permitted, in being "scrupulously" faithful about asking for things and in "leaving all decisions to Mother", is happily easing out of popularity as an ideal. A much better practice than leaving all things to Mother would be to make some decisions of my own about traveling light. A superior should be able to presume that when a subject asks for something, that religious has already made a private act of judgment as to whether she really needs it and has come humbly seeking the fulfillment of what she considers to be a genuine need. True, the poor religious must be prepared to receive or to be refused with equal good grace, and out of a predetermined act of submission of will. But this is far different than the mentality that makes no private evaluations and comes to no personal decisions, considering that just to ask for anything and everything is the epitome of poverty. Actually it is a lazy-minded poverty and a poverty calculated to encourage an unthinkingness that will carry over into other areas of religious life and produce at best a well-functioning robot and at worst a numb-brained yes-man.

There is communal poverty, for which the superior is primarily but by no means solely responsible. There is also that matter of each religious having made his own vow of poverty. With the pronouncement of the vow has come the responsibility of fulfilling the vow. And responsibility always presupposes thought, judgment, and decision. Whether or not the superior concurs in the subject's thought, judgment, or decision in particular cases alters nothing of the subject's responsibility to carry on these private processes. Young religious should be taught to confer first of all with themselves about needs. In more important matters it may be appropriate to do some specific soliciting of the Holy Spirit for light on the matter. In all matters the poor religious should be daily making decisions about his poverty, at least in the basic sense of being each day deliberately poor and with the consciousness that his vow is his own and that he alone can keep it; he alone can grow in the perfection of the virtue that belongs to *his* vow.

It has been well said that religious chastity is a vow to love. It can also be said that Franciscan poverty is a vow to have the littlest measure of things and the greatest measure of joy. The Rule of the monks of Taizé contains a splendid Franciscan declaration: "The spirit of poverty is to live in the gladness of today." We remember that our holy Father Francis had this against the ant: it is too preoccupied with tomorrow.

All of this does not pretend to supply answers to painfully complex questions about poverty in modern religious life. It merely offers a few suggestions. But one is probably justifiably insistent in maintaining that genuine Franciscan joy cannot carry heavy personal luggage if it is to give its open embrace to the poor of the earth. Our blessed Father Francis objected that to have property would necessitate having weapons to defend it, and there are obvious present analogies. Who has not seen the little pistols of irritability and the hand grenades of petulance with which a religious will defend his small citadel of supposed needs, conveniences, and arrangements? Saint Francis wandered over the earth after the manner of the young heir inspecting with satisfaction his Father's property. And that is just what he was. He never needed to grasp things. For he had really understood that in having nothing he possessed all things, and that whatever he needed would be given him in that hour.

VII   *The Mount of Vision*

Recently an applicant asked me about "blind obedience" and "wise obedience". "What's the difference?" she
wanted to know. We could make some interesting speculations about what sort of philosophical or spiritual climate makes it possible for an intelligent woman to ask such
a question in all gravity and sincerity. We might comment
on the uncommonly good press superficiality is enjoying
these days. We could attack past abuses of authority. We
might get very excited and make a speech about personal
responsibility and individual freedom. But meanwhile the
applicant is waiting for an answer.

In the present-day occupation with accenting the concept of *person* with all its healthy ramifications of freedom, dignity, and individual charisms, there is probably
no term so well calculated to set every stew pot in the

discussion circle boiling and every printer's pan sizzling as "blind obedience". Mention this and picket lines rise up like genii. Flags fly. Cannons boom. The war is on. And the combatants want no truce or treaty. Unconditional victory is, at least in this area, enthusiastically desired. "Obedience is supposed to keep its eyes open. Blind obedience is for pre-Council fossils."

The trouble with these two statements taken as an entity is that they present us with that most insidious of lies: the half-truth. For true obedience decidedly does have its eyes open. But blind obedience is and always was— for no one.

The term "blind obedience" is, along with "particular friendship" and "self-love", one of those misnomers which has persisted through the centuries, often a cause of misunderstanding and confusion and sometimes a source of anguish, especially to young religious. Certainly every genuine friendship is by its nature particular. It is strange that so eminently descriptive a term should have been fastened on the grotesque alliance in which two persons engage in a reciprocal devouring process. Again, we know that Christ made it quite plain that we must have a rightly ordered love for ourselves when he gave us this love as the norm of our love for our fellows: "Love your neighbor as yourself." Yet, how many venerable tomes have warned us about "self-love" until the term has become synonymous for many a religious with all that precludes her growing in holiness. Self-will, too. Is not my self's will the only will I have? What other will may I claim except my own? It is a pity that we have come down the centuries brandishing verbal clubs against self-love and self-will when we rather obviously really meant psycho-logical gluttony and self-commitment to the extent of self-circumscription.

This same type of shallow thinking has fixed on two antitheses and presented them as an integral unit. At one pole is that servility which is indigenous to the lazy brain, the irresolute will, the obsequious mentality. At the other pole is that clear-eyed faith which sturdily believes that God can "accomplish" more through one fully human act of submission than through the operation of all the human talents in the world, the faith that understands that it is not always necessary to see reasons so long as one sees God. These pure antitheses are coupled under a doubly false caption: blind obedience. Actually, the first is not obedience at all. The second is the most clear-sighted obedience there is.

In number 14, *Perfectae Caritatis* speaks of that profes-sion of obedience by which the "religious offer the full surrender of their own will as a sacrifice of themselves to God". Now, every sacrifice carries the connotation of offering and consummation. It often denotes smoke and blood. It is too urgent for afternoon tea and too vital for the cocktail lounge. We shall have to keep sacrifice in its proper context, which is giving, if we are to understand at all what Vatican II has to say to us about obedience.

It is often faith alone that can lend meaning to our giving, and it is faith that fires the love which inspires sacrifice. How splendidly this faith shone in our founder Saint Francis! "I would obey a novice of one day if he were appointed my superior", the seraphic father declared. It may be very important for us to pause in the midst of

our dialogues and discussions to ask ourselves a pertinent
question: "Would I?"

There is today a very healthy disdain for the sometimes notion that the "grace of office" is an everflowing
fountain that rinses from the superior any possible defects
left over from the days she was a subject, or a funnel
inserted in her head for letting in the illuminations from
on high that supply for the lack of sense. It is no longer
thought reasonable to suppose that holding office is an
ex opere operato, automatic affair that transforms incompetence into ability. However, in these healthy rejec-
tions, there is also the seed of destruction as regards
obedience. We want to watch for it. For obedience is
not a matter of carrying out the superior's decisions or
requests because we consider her wise and the decisions
well taken. This is to reduce obedience to a purely natural plane, uprooting it theologically and actually rob-
bing it of its identity.

To subscribe to the superior's views when they happen to coincide with my own is action scarcely meriting
the dignity to be called obedience. In the very first line
of its section on obedience, *Perfectae Caritatis* sets down
the truth of the matter with unequivocal exactness: "In
professing obedience, religious offer the full surrender of
their own will as a sacrifice of themselves to God and so
are united permanently and securely to God's salvific will"
(no. 14).

It needs to be brought to the attention of young religious and held before the eyes of the elders that the "full
surrender" of will made at profession is a continuing self-
donation according to the nature of human surrender that

cannot be made once and forever but must be constantly renewed. Just as a woman after marriage may fully surrender her person to her husband and later withdraw her giving, so can a religious make a magnificent act of surrender of will at her profession only to renege in her giving afterward. This is self-evident. It is, in fact, part of the fickleness of human nature that each should tend to do this. The unhappiness and unrest manifest in so many areas of religious life today are often clearly the result of failure to surrender *fully* and *constantly* to God. A vow of obedience is not a matter of making a decision but of engaging oneself in a lifetime of personal decisions. I must each day anew and even in every varying situation *decide* to obey. It is *my* vow, which no one can observe for me. It is a question of *my* surrender, which no one else in the world can make but me.

According as the surrender of one's will as a sacrifice to God is limited, unhappiness is increased. We cannot honestly say, "I love you with all my heart!" while fisting away a good portion of the heart for ourselves. We are always insecure when we are only half-given. When our involvement with our vow of obedience is so superficial and precarious that we become disengaged from our commitment by a mere wind of human unreasonableness or a squall of human frustration, we have not the sense of inner permanence so essential to genuine peace. Scripture loves to compare the religious man to a tree planted by running waters. There is no denying that scorching winds blow against most if not all religious at one time or another, that months and perhaps years of drought assail the tree with their threat of destruction. But to have stretched out one's roots into the stream of God's salvific will is to be a tree that survives the winds and stays green in drought.

Perfectae Caritatis makes this clear: "And so [they] are united permanently and securely to God's salvific will" (no. 14). No other way. In partial surrender, in reserved obedience, lies the sense of impermanence and insecurity that tortures many a religious today. There is, after all, no real permanence without God "changeless and true". He is our only authentic security. If "obedience" is held as a rationalization process, it cannot produce permanence or security, for these dearly prized treasures can never be anything but ephemeral, tenuous, and evanescent outside God.

Saint Francis has not been recorded as saying that he did not care a snap whether the wisest elder brother or the most unformed novice was his superior. He is not on record as putting the most unlikely human material into the chair of Moses so that divine illuminations could be more unmistakable. But he did say that *if* a novice were made his superior, he would obey him. His reason was not that the novice would have annexed all wisdom and understanding on the day of his installation as superior, but simply that the novice had been installed as superior.

This was to be the normal situation, then: a superior with good hearing, ready to listen, and full of love and compassion; a subject without fear either to speak or to submit. "The Lord often reveals what is better to the lesser ones", wrote the seraphic foundress in her Rule. Before we become *too* facile in talking of their "medieval

mentality", we shall want to ponder the curiously con-
temporary ring of so many of their words. Yet, with all
their insistence on openness, as when Saint Clare instructs
the abbess to confer at chapter with *all* her daughters
about whatever concerns the common good, and as when
Saint Francis asks his friars, "Does it seem good to you
that I should do that?" and then reverses his personal
decision, Clare and Francis were always equipped for the
extraordinary situation. They had made a *full* surrender
of themselves to God in sacrifice and were permanently
and securely united to God's salvific will (see PC, no. 14).
They were thus mature enough to practice the obedience necessary in a crisis situation. "I would obey a novice of one day if he were appointed my superior."

It is astonishing sometimes how little we seem able to
establish any sense of communication with Christ in personal "obedience crises". Christ's earthly superiors were
an uncommonly sorry lot. Certainly we have all medi-
tated on his respectful replies to spiritual pygmies, his
genteelness with the fawning sycophant of the high priest,
his docility before ambition-ridden Caiphas and inhumane Annas. These things happen. Small-souled men do
sometimes become superiors. Ambition still feeds upon
itself today even as it cancerously devours its very asso-
ciates. Such situations are tragic for such superiors. The
same situations may be sufferingly glorious for the subjects. And they *are* extraordinary. It is probably the dreary
situation that provokes rebellion and abandonment of the
religious life more than the scandalous one. Most persons
can suffer abuse better than incompetence. Still, the "full
surrender of their own will as a sacrifice of themselves to

God" is perhaps more blessed in God's eyes when repeated in dreariness than bannered in tragedy.

Saint Francis was refused a bishop's permission to preach in his episcopal precincts. The bishop ought not to have acted like that. People knew Francis was a saint. Jealous of his rights, that bishop! Probably a crochety old authoritarian of no vision who mistrusted anything new. A conservative? Likely enough. For Francis was highly unconservative in the sense that he was always so intent on conserving the core of spiritual reality that he had necessarily to put aside masses of meaningless trivia. Or maybe the bishop was even a traditionalist! For Francis was just not the traditional kind of preacher, to say nothing of the traditional type of founder of a religious Order. And Saint Francis, totally dedicated to God and souls, sought no profit, asked only to spend himself on the people of God. The situation is clear by the simplest rationalization process. Probably the action to be taken in the situation would be equally clear to some persons today. However, the fact is that Saint Francis did not picket the bishop.

He took action, though. He wouldn't accept this lying down. So, he went around to the back door, which he probably considered a more appropriate entrance for the fourth-class merchandise he felt himself to be, and tried again. He did get in. And he did preach. And he probably did quite a bit for the bishop. We only wish we knew more about that bishop, instead of just having to make pleasant conjectures about how he probably went out and started a credit union on the south side of town and began to dialogue energetically with young curates.

Perfectae Caritatis reminds us that "Jesus Christ . . . learned obedience in the school of suffering" (no. 14). We cannot hope to learn it elsewhere. While dialogue between superior and subject is the normal atmosphere in which obedience should operate, and whereas discussion groups can be wonderfully effective in enlarging our concept of obedience and affording us new insights, still it is not in dialogue or discussion or self-development programs that we learn it. This graduate study can be made only in one school, that of suffering. Does not real sacrifice of its nature involve suffering? Abraham was fit to become the father of a great people not through wondrously begetting a son in his wife's old age, but because he was ready to obey the most inhumane and unreasonable command that he kill that son. Rightly should we call the scene of such obedience the Mount of Vision. The Mount of Blind Obedience is not its name.

Who of us has not personally witnessed the marvels God works through that obedience which suffers in faith? Out of the most humanly untoward situations God initiates religious Orders, establishes new foundations, raises up fresh enterprises, and sanctifies the souls of his own.

It is patently true that in the past there has often been far too little attention accorded the dignity of the individual charisms. Surely superiors must be aware that the talents of those in their communities are clues as to the manner in which God wants to be served by these individuals. He does not give his gifts by mistake or happenstance. Still, when all due praise is accorded the healthier atmosphere of the present and all merited enthusiasm exhibited for the development of personalities and

gifts and talents and charisms, we must return to the basic
meaning of obedience: a full *surrender* of self as a *sacrifice*
to God. Speaking of religious who "under the motion
of the Holy Spirit subject themselves in faith to their
superiors who hold the place of God", *Perfectae Caritatis*,
in number 14, shows us the result of such subjection:
"*So* they are closely bound to the service of the Church
and strive to attain the measure of the full manhood of
Christ (Eph. 4:13)." *So.* Not by the measure of their
accomplishments do they serve the Church, but by the
measure of their faith. But do not the Scriptures say that
faith without works is dead? They do indeed. It is indeed.
But we want to remember that submission is work. It is
proving too arduous a work for some these days.

"I, little brother Francis, promise obedience." There
is a kind of personal manifesto in these familiar words of
our father and founder. I, the insignificant one, the lesser
servant of the people of God. I, the one related to everyone in brotherhood. I myself, Francis. I make my glorious commitment. I promise obedience. The important
thing about a promise is that we keep it. The really touching thing about a promise is that even when we break it
we still desire to keep it.

It is admirable to consume our ink supply in spelling
out freedom in all scripts so long as we know what freedom is. Religious "should use both the forces of their
intellect and will and the gifts of nature and grace", insists
Perfectae Caritatis in words calculated to warm the heart
of your local editor. It is just the way that sentence ends
that may be disconcerting to some: "... to execute the
commands and fulfill the duties entrusted to them [by

superiors]." Vatican II wants a deliberate obedience. This is the way Saint Francis envisioned it. He simply *wanted* to obey. He decided to obey, and he kept on making decisions until he died.

Young religious must not be allowed to build up false concepts of obedience. It is not a ticket that entitles you to remain in this institution, eat its meals, and do its work. It is not a necessary price to pay for remaining in the establishment. It is first an act of maturity and then a continued functioning of maturity in repeated choices and decisions. Saint Francis chose to obey when obedience was pleasant. He decided to obey when obedience was painful. "I, little brother Francis, promise obedience." "I, Clare, prostrate at the feet of Holy Church. . . ." Here are two personalities that were not exactly flattened by obedience, which sometimes struck at the very core of their hearts. Saint Francis was not reduced to neutral matter by keeping his promise to obey, come whatever weather. Saint Clare obviously did not grow into a pretzel by remaining prostrate at the feet of Holy Church.

In an address to women religious in 1962,[1] Blessed Pope John XXIII urged that superiors "make obedience sweet". This is not the same as to make it always easy. Hard things are often sweet to do, providing we love the person for whom we do them. Only the subject can make it easy in a certain sense, and this by faith in full surrender of self. "But, if one passes from the respect of the person to the exaltation of the personality and to the affirmation of personalism, the dangers become serious",

[1] "Il Tempio Massimo", Exhortation to Women Religious, July 2, 1962.

warned Pope John in that same address. And he showed himself the herald of the Decree on the renewal of religious life (*Perfectae Caritatis*), with its forthright acknowledgment that obedience is learned in the school of suffering when he added, "This constant sacrifice of your 'ego', this annihilation of self can cost much, but it is also true that herein lies the victory, for heavenly graces correspond to this spiritual crucifixion for you and for all humanity." It is I alone who can keep my promise of obedience. But I keep it on behalf of all the people of God and to their credit.

VIII   *The Religious Family*

A vocation, unlike an angel, is not pure spirit without body. Vocations come packaged in human persons. It is strange that in this era of such heavy underscorings of *person*, we still speak so frequently of *vocations* as though of disembodied responses to a call.

There is not, after all, question of a "call" but of someone called. If there is at present a crisis in this area, it is not a "vocation crisis". For vocations do not have crises—people do. "Are you getting vocations?" we inquire of Orders and congregations. Of course, they are not. They never did. They received persons with vocations. And one of the several reasons that we may not be getting so many persons with vocations now is that we have handled both pre-entrance and post-entrance persons with something of that statistical approach so dear to the American mentality. We are the world's most enthusiastic survey takers, graphers, and pollsters. This talent will inevitably make its presence known in areas where it is actually better not exercised—such as in the mystery of community life.

How many "vocations" are coming into religious houses has no particular meaning of itself. In fact, nowhere are numbers per se more misleading. "Too many friars minor," mourned our Father Saint Francis, "too many friars minor! Would that the world could marvel at their fewness." On the other hand, the caliber of persons presently attracted to the religious life and what it is that attracts them (that is, what instrumentality God's grace uses to attract them) are extremely important. However, we cannot directly measure the compulsion of hearts. For this is required the Divine Statistician, the Holy Spirit.

More important still, in humbly probing the mystery of community life, is the attempt to discover what holds people in religious life. God's grace, to be sure—but God's grace made manifest in human love. For altogether too long we have used this "vocation" phraseology instead of the phraseology of person. We have good vocations, or we lack vocations. We are losing vocations, or we are getting vocations. Even that expression "getting" betrays a certain poverty of concept. Communities are not recruiting centers where we "get" vocations. Rather, communities are meant to be the capital cities in God's kingdom of love into whose warm citizenry we receive young people who are to be fed upon this love and thus become strong to contribute to this love.

Our blessed Lord did not recruit twelve vocations. He called twelve men, one of whom apostatized from his indubitably authentic vocation. That a true vocation can be lost, a sure call fail after a time to evoke a continuing response is thus evident from the beginning of community life in the Church. Happily, there is today a strong pull away from the concept of disembodiment. However, as might be expected with strong pulls on an old rope, a number of persons have pulled so hard at the idea of "person" as contraposed to the idea of "vocation" that they have fallen over backward.

One evidence of this has already been discussed: the personal fulfillment cult. The reaction against certain and perhaps even prolific past errors of allowing the God-given talents of religious to atrophy, or in some few areas even attempting to stifle them as though the gifts of God were something to be held in suspicion if found in a religious, must not be the establishing of a personality cult. Nor may we attribute this preoccupation with self-fulfillment to the type of young persons casting convent-ward glances these days as though they themselves had initiated it. Youth is invariably characterized by a great desire to give. When this becomes a desire to get, it is usually because those who should have supplied inspiration to youth have failed. When not enough is asked of young people, they tend to become lethargic about giving anything. The high idealism of "How much can I give?" degenerates easily enough into the familiar "What's in it for me?"

Actually, even when we have driven youth to such a substratum approach to life, all is not lost. We can still come up at the eleventh vocational hour (which the present hour may well be) and give at last the right answer to the wrong question. "What's in religious life for me?" It is up to us if we are going to answer by way of our own manner of living: "Why!—membership in a reputable club and complete social security." Or it is our decision whether we shall say: "What's in it for you?—Why, a chance to spend yourself on God and his people, to empty yourself and wear yourself out and give every ounce of your love and your energy until you are ushered into eternal rest!" It may make a great difference in the quality of subjects we receive how we decide to answer that question. It may also make a great difference whether we communicate to young people the attitude and atmosphere of giving or of getting after they have entered religious life.

It is a heinous crime to deprive youth of its need to sacrifice itself in love for a great ideal. We need take no pains to explain to young people that one is automatically fulfilled by giving oneself to others. They experience this. Maybe we are talking too much about these things. It requires considerable imaginational gymnastics to picture Saint Francis pondering his personal fulfillment. He was, for one thing, too busy. Like all the saints, he became a perfectly fulfilled person, but it is a safe wager that he never once in his religious life gave a thought to personal fulfillment. True personal fulfillment is a natural phenomenon of sacrificial love that occurs, not a course of action that has to be planned.

The community always needs to grow in the consciousness, however, that it is receiving not vocations but persons whom it believes to have vocations. Thus, when we receive a young subject into religious life, we receive her as she is. We agree to accept her (and this in the sense of receive, not in the sense of tolerate) with all her deficiencies, her blind spots, her rough edges, as well as with her gifts, her talents, and her charm. Then, during the novitiate period, we endeavor with the gentle instruments of love, compassion, and inspiration to educate the young religious in the ways of self-knowledge that will make her both aware of curable deficiencies and appreciative of curative measures, which will bring increasing vision into the blind spots and soften the rough edges in the way that water wears away the sharpness of a stone rather than after the fashion of a pumice or a file.

We discourse so much these days on community as an institution to be improved, whereas it is really a mystery of love to be pondered. "Common life", says *Perfectae Caritatis*, is "fashioned on the model of the early Church where the body of believers was united in heart and soul (cf. Acts 4:32), and given new force by the teaching of the Gospel, the sacred liturgy and especially the Eucharist" (no. 15). The document adds that community life should "continue to be lived in prayer and the communion of the same spirit." "Communion" appears to be the key word in that final phrase. How truly it has been said that community life and community spirit are learned by osmosis. We do not teach love and unity; we communicate them. We establish them as an atmosphere. We preach them by our attitude without noise of words.

"The community", continues *Perfectae Caritatis*, "[as] a true family gathered together in the name of the Lord by God's love which has flooded the hearts of its members through the Holy Spirit (cf. Rom. 5:5), rejoices because He is present among them (cf. Matt. 18:20)." It will be quite useless to instruct young religious in charity if we do not offer them an atmosphere of charity in which to study and to grow. We cannot delineate the ideals of the Order or congregation so as to inspire real efforts to attain them if our novices are not able to see those ideals incarnated in the professed religious. This is not to say that all professed religious must be or even could be perfect incarnations of the ideals of their institute. But it is to maintain that the true incarnation of an ideal is quite readily recognizable by the terrible perspicacity of youth even when it sees only a very imperfect incarnational setting. Young religious are seldom repelled by human weakness. They are always repulsed by falseness.

A rewarding paradox of community life is that the more we are concerned with maintaining in love the union in heart and soul of which *Perfectae Caritatis* speaks, the less need we have to be taken up with uniformity of action. Such quasi-uniformity as is necessary for upholding the discipline always proper to a religious house seems spontaneously to appear out of the unity of hearts that prevails among the religious. And this may be our surest guiding norm about how much external uniformity is desirable.

As with the vocation-versus-person problems of the past that have generated the extremism of the personality cultists, so the chafing of many persons under rigid external uniformity can produce a certain spirit of anarchy in regard to all external discipline. We need to work down to the roots of the situation. Where uniformity per se has been the ideal, we shall not be surprised to discover present-day youth rejecting it and even rebelling against it. They are justified, for such uniformity is false and contrived. We shall never supply for a lack of the holy and meaningful unity, which is the unity of hearts and souls in a common love of God and one another under a common inspiration, by an imposed uniformity of performance. Equally untenable, however, is the position that all uniformity is undesirable and an indication of rigidity. This is, in fact, not so much position as posturing.

An angular external discipline in a religious house whose life is not arched with love can be only forbidding, a hollow and brittle thing. There is, nonetheless, a certain uniformity that issues out of unity, and to deny this is to attack the validity of that very spontaneity our age is so eager to defend. Because there may have been a tendency in the past to prize uniformity for its own sake and even as an end, we can presently become nervous and self-conscious about any uniformity at all. I do not, after all, have to wind my veil into a turban to prove I am a free adult religious woman and not enslaved to institutional uniformity. It would be rather a pity if I could not conceptually isolate my sense of personal identity except by studiously doing the opposite of the nun in the next choir stall. There is no particular reason based on faith, morals, or radical religious discipline why nuns in choir cannot cradle their breviaries on their knees and read from them with their heads propped on bent elbow supports, nor for that matter that they cannot cross their knees or even put their feet up on the stalls. But it would be altogether too sad if I had to adopt one of these departures from the traditional uniformity of holding my breviary with dignity in order to prove I have not been made grist for the mill of the establishment.

It is noticeable both in history and on the testimony of current events that the really great independent spirits did not fret and chafe about uniformity but understood it as a sometimes-valid expression of unity, an all-times very minor part of realism, and a no-times ultimate goal.

Unity of hearts and souls in a religious community does not and should not produce uniformity of taste any more than it produces uniformity of complexion, height, or girth. The superior who attempts to form her community according to her own preferences in nonessentials is obviously aborting her sisters' growth according to the spirit as well as according to nature since the former raises its edifice on the latter. On the other hand, it is perfectly normal and to be expected that the superior will leave her mark on the community and that the members will be in some way influenced by her tastes. We shall seldom see a monastery or convent that does not reflect either the artistic bad taste or good taste of the superior, and there is surely no need to begin inveighing against structure, establishment, and maternalism because this is so.

In our praiseworthy efforts to underscore the individual these days, we must be aware of the hazard of community self-consciousness, which threatens us. There has certainly been in some quarters of religious life in the past a paternalism and maternalism calculated to keep adult persons at child level. We want to recognize and deplore this and to take the measures readily enough indicated that such situations do not occur or recur. However, we do not want to fly into a nervous frenzy about it, so that we declare the natural to be the contrived and condemn normalcy as neurosis.

We may notice a specific peculiarity in this field as regards emotion. We are talking a very great deal about love these days. This is all very good, so long as we are loving as well as talking. But it is strange how suspicious we sometimes become of the perfectly normal manifestations of love. We deplore the sometimes lack of communication between superiors and subjects in the past and the loveless relationship between them. Yet, when we discover unmistakable evidence of warm affection between them, we can swoop down upon these manifestations with loud cries of "Maternalism!" and "Infantilism!" It is probably only part of the larger and familiar picture of well-meaning persons hopelessly or at least helplessly entangled today in jargon. We can go to quite elaborate lengths to prepare the accoutrements of an agape meal in a religious house only to become very agitated if the community exhibits any emotion over the illness of the superior, her temporary departure from them, the surprises she prepares for them.

We seem especially nervous about tears, as though there were something undignified in them. To be sure, tears can be undignified in the same way that laughter can. It all depends on the person who sheds them or raises it. Nothing is so mawkish and degrading in a grown person as sentimental, infantile tears, unless it is hollow and forced laughter. *Perfectae Caritatis* speaks of the community as a true family in which love has flooded the hearts of the members. Now, a flood is by its nature something that overflows the banks. Smiles of pleasure, frowns of disappointment, tears in sorrow or poignancy—these are part of the apparatus of love, to be always controlled but never condemned. It is poor taste to wear one's heart on one's sleeve. It is poor Christianity to wear one's heart under a bulletproof vest of subemotionality. The great stone face is not the face of Christ.

The heart-flooding love of which *Perfectae Caritatis* speaks will necessarily produce by its irrigation all which is proper to united hearts: shared joys and shared sorrows, deep and sincere interest in one another, real concern for one another. Perhaps we must acknowledge a certain tendency in the past to fail in inculcating a family spirit among our young members by an oversolicitude for their emotional and spiritual equilibrium so that we were eager to share all the joys of community with them but solicitous to spare them the sorrows of community life.

Actually, young people do not generally react gratefully to such overprotectiveness. It is certainly true that postulants and novices have a right to expect inspiration from the older members and that the professed religious have a duty to provide incarnational inspiration for the beginners in religious life. But if this is done unselfconsciously and is simply a natural issue of sincerely supernatural living, the young will be prepared to look with compassion on weakness and with acceptance on occasional aberrations. It is anyhow useless to be perpetually trying to hide from the young the obvious deficiencies in the community. Every family has its sorrows, and religious families are no exception. *Perfectae Caritatis* reminds us that the members of a religious family are "to bear each other's burdens", and normally high-minded and idealistic young religious are more content and more gratified to be allowed to help bear the elders' burdens than to be fenced off from them.

It is important in the normal process of maturation that belongs to the whole period of religious formation that the young religious have that advantage of true family life which arises from the intermingling of age groups. How many times has it happened in the past that novices, kept in strict isolation from all the religious save their own group, are then cast out after profession into a more normal family grouping in which they find themselves quite lost. Again let us agree that it will always be desirable to have postulants and novices separated in some sense from the professed religious, but we suspect there has been too much rigor in the interpretation of this separation in the past.

Cloisters admittedly have an advantage here. Because of their architectural smallness as well as due to their always limited numbers in relation to the institutions of active apostolate, there will be of necessity a closer bond between age groups. This is a boon they will not want to lose. One can usually determine the caliber of a community by its general attitude toward the aged. Where the retired elders are held in genuine esteem by the young, the little eccentricities of old age regarded with indulgent affection, and the sense of communal indebtedness to the aged fostered, and where the exuberant junior members are warmly cherished by the aged, their extravagances accepted, and their rawness clothed with understanding—there we have community. There also we have that "source of great apostolic energy" to which *Perfectae Caritatis* refers.

No one will deny that love is the most energizing force in the world. We forget exhaustion; we forget ourselves in an effort to please one who has made us important by his love for us, but are languid and apathetic when unsparked by affection. We are full of ideas when we are loved and loving, dull when we seem unappreciated and unwanted.

One of our difficulties about communal recreation that has led to the presently exaggerated emphasis on the "hobby groups" may be that we have tried to simulate an interest in the uninteresting *interests* of others and have failed miserably, whereas we really needed only to be interested in *others* to have succeeded gloriously in plotting out a vast acreage of conviviality. We can certainly not always be interested in what another religious says, but we can always be interested in that religious. The idea is family. Community. Mystery of love.

In a stirring reference to Saint John, *Perfectae Caritatis* declares that "the unity of the brethren is a visible pledge that Christ will return" (no. 15). Blessed Dom Columba Marmion has remarked that the love that reigns among the members of a community is the surest sign of Christ's protection of that community. There is no need then to be nervous about community, to be self-conscious or agitated in examining communal life, prepared to shout, "Structure!" if someone opens a door for the superior, or to cry, "Maternalism!" if the superior acknowledges the love of her daughters with a smart under her eyelids. Who would dare call Saint Clare maternalistic when she crept about cold San Damiano at night to make sure her sleeping daughters were properly blanketed? Or who would presume to execrate the relationship between Saint Francis and Brother Leo, "little sheep of God", as precious or darling instead of beautifully virile?

What a moving picture of community life our Franciscan forebears offer us! And what psychological balance it displayed! We find them convivial and eremetical, singing and laughing and praying together and going to caves alone, conscious each of his separate identity (and how differently Francis dealt with the many personalities God put under his care and fostering) and of his part in community. Above all, the Franciscans of the Eden days of the Order were completely natural in their supernatural living. Quite a few serpentine ideas have slithered into that Eden, but the love which floods the hearts of the members (see PC, no. 15) of Francis' and Clare's numerous progeny can still drown any number of snakes.

Saint Francis cried because "Love is not loved", he "bleated" with tenderness at Greccio's crib, he fiddled with two sticks to relieve his joy, he sang because he had a Father in heaven, he asked for almond cookies in his last illness, and he got an angel to play the violin for him when such revelry was considered inappropriate by the friars. Completely unaffected, Francis found laughter and tears equally valid functions of the love that flooded his heart. He was a superior so perfect as to share with his subjects the simple awareness of his own imperfections. He was a genuine community man.

IX   *Not to Be Served, but to Serve*

At the end of the ceremonies of solemn vows for a Poor Clare nun, the bishop turns from the last blessing over the newly professed and gives the abbess a large assignment. "Take this spouse of Jesus Christ under your care and direction", he commands. Then he enjoins two other directives: "Keep her consecrated and present her spotless to God, knowing that you must render an account for her before the tribunal of her Spouse, the future judge."

Now, each of us has at least one talent for running in the wrong direction or even in several directions at once. Some have five talents for this. There are those who have ten. We would none of us be so foolish as to deny that even consecrated souls have a facility for performing quite unconsecratedly in trying circumstances. And it is often difficult to fight off the depression that comes of seeing how frightfully spotty we are. It seems our outstanding annexation as we trudge along the way of perfection is—more spots.

So how, precisely, does one little human being take such care of another person and direct her so surely that she remains stable in consecration and at death offers the angels a spotless burden to sweep up to God? Even God refuses to impose his omnipotence on the human will, which he has created free. So, it is immediately clear that the superior is not set to "make" a sister holy. Her love and solicitude and her example are not meant to be a kind of spiritual spot remover. It must rather be that by her humility before the deep and delicate mystery that each person is, the superior is in some way to identify herself with her subjects, and by her compassionate under-standing of them inspire in them a desire to relinquish the muddy comfort of spots in favor of the only effective cleansing agent, which is the love of God.

Number 14 of *Perfectae Caritatis* is quite in accord with the above-quoted injunction of the ritual, as are both with the words of Saint Paul in Hebrews 13:17, in saying that superiors are "those who are to give an account of the souls entrusted to them". And it continues that, because of such an accounting to be made to such a Higher Superior, earthly superiors "should fulfill their office in a way responsive to God's will." This is actually to say that their best methodology in the direction of souls is no human methodology at all but a personal open-ness to God.

If anyone in a community is threatened with the clut-tering of soul that multiple concerns can engender, it is the superior. Yet, it is precisely the superior who must above all remain uncluttered in soul so that the inspirations of grace may find her accessible rather than occupied. And so God gives superiors a precious gift to accelerate the emptying-out process. It is the prize of helplessness before souls.

It is certainly necessary and perhaps even imperative that a superior have a firm understanding and working knowledge of the psychology of human behavior. She needs to know psychological principles, and she must have the tact to apply them availingly. She has to learn by experience how theories of typical human behavior patterns appear in practice. And a valid religious existentialism must vitalize the classicism of her principles. Yet, with all of these, plus possible high intelligence and even wisdom, she will invariably experience the human helplessness of one person confronted by the mystery of another person. In this very realization of her limitations and even powerlessness, the superior should find her realest security.

It is needful to experience one's finitude in order to be prepared for the influx of Infinitude that one who holds office and has been given the care of souls has every right to expect from God. If, however, the superior hopes to find within herself even the means to cope with all situations, much less the wisdom to deal with souls, she is already militating against her own and the community's spiritual interests. A servant is essentially a dependent. We shall preserve ourselves from mere glibness about service and ministry if we seriously ponder the dependent state that superiorship indicates.

A superior never knows what is coming next. She, more than any of her sisters, *must* live from hour to hour, intent upon God and utterly dependent upon him. It is desirable that an abbess have qualities of leadership, but it is essential that she have a sense of dependence and servitude. All her education and experience and even all her prayer and her spirituality should serve only to accentuate her awareness of her dependence upon God. There is no conceptual conflict between the idea of a superior giving herself utterly to her community and the idea of the superior's obligation to give only Christ to the community. She can live in the happy awareness that she can do all things *in* Christ. But she finds her security in the realization that she can do nothing at all *out of* Christ. And what do we mean by "in" Christ, if not that she has plunged her entire being into Christ? He is not "with" her, but she is "in" him. In this awareness of her mission to serve, and of service as dependence, the superior discovers her special vocation to poverty.

The abbess ought to keep nothing of herself for herself. Her health, her energy, her time, her talent, her love are to be squandered upon the sisters. "They should exercise their authority out of a spirit of service to the brethren, expressing in this way the love with which God loves their subjects" (PC, no. 14). And how does God love them? "He so loved the world as to give his only-begotten Son" (Jn 3:16). He "emptied himself, taking the form of a servant" (Phil 2:7). He "came not to be served but to serve" (Mt 20:28).

Canon law tells us how old the superior should be. Constitutions will let us know how long she needs to have been professed. But since maturity is a relative and highly subjective matter, sometimes quite disproportionate to either age or religious experience, and since we may seek dispensations in the matters of both age and profession, we shall want immediately to look far beyond these relativisms to find the absolutisms to be sought in a superior.

Let us look at two superiors who were most faithful servants, who left a mark not only on their communities, but on the world society even to our own day: Saint Francis and Saint Clare. Here are two totally committed persons. But they are committed to God and community not with the outthrust mental jaw of some modern "committants", but with the easy joy of the children of God. Healthwise, neither was a very imposing physical specimen. Francis was a slight man who had stomach trouble and increasingly poor vision. Clare had nearly invalided herself by early indiscretions in austerity, which fact doubtless caused her much chagrin and humiliation later on, and to wish she had had a superior instead of being one. Their mental health, however, was indeed imposing. Their emotional health was exuberant. Is this not what we must look for in choosing superiors?

Clare and Francis were utterly real. They laughed and they wept; they became depressed and they grew ecstatic. They were capable of extravagance (Saint Francis' hilarity was not always appreciated by some of his staid sons) and of high-handedness (Saint Clare told the friars that if they could not instruct her nuns in the spiritual life, they could just keep their food, too!). They made mistakes (Clare damaged her health, and Francis imposed

too harsh a penance on Brother Rufino), which they
acknowledged. They never attempted to create an authority image and were obviously not preoccupied with their
positions. It was their wonderful humanity and their
healthy approach to the world as well as to God that
created for them and for us an image of warm, accessible love.

"I also beg the one who will be in the service of the
sisters that she strive to lead the way for the others more
by her virtues and holy way of acting than by her office,
so that roused by her example the sisters may obey her
not so much because of her office but more out of love"
(Testament of Saint Clare). Certainly Saint Clare was centuries ahead not only of her own time, but of all the
ensuing hard-lipped eras that canonized "dutiful" obedience when she wrote those shocking words! Too often
obedience has been presented to young religious as a matter of setting your lips, lowering your head, and bravely
pushing on toward misery's eternal reward, this latter being
the only pleasant concept related to obedience. *Perfectae
Caritatis* specifically, however, enjoins on the superior the
duty to make subordination of the will easier for subjects. This is entirely in accord with the spirit of Saint
Francis and Saint Clare. How many treatises of unreal
spirituality have delineated the superior as a dour power
figure set to make subjects holy by breaking their wills
and flattening their humanity. In fact, the more remote
and uncharming the superior is, the better for the subjects, who will thus grow more sturdily in faith, detach-
ment, and corresponding inhumanity (though this last area
of growth was, understandably, not mentioned).

Saint Clare was aware that love, like service, must be not only exercised but experienced. A woman simply cannot be fully herself unless she is loved. And the religious superior of women remains herself a woman with the same basic needs of womanhood felt by her sisters. It is a very good thing that we are so conscious these days of the subject's need to be loved. It is rather widely overlooked, however, that the superior also needs to be loved. A potentially excellent leader can be rendered powerless by the incooperativeness or disloyalty of those she is set to lead. An essentially lovable superior can be limited in her expression of love because she is not loved. There is, as a matter of fact, nothing quite so emotionally debilitating for a superior as to have her love rejected. And the rejection and disloyalty of the few can weaken the superior's contribution to the many. An unloved woman cannot give herself fully for the simple reason that she is rendered less herself by being unloved. This is equally true of the religious woman, superior as well as sister.

No superior can fully exercise her office of servant unless her service is wanted and (at least ultimately) valued. Service necessarily implies not only a servant, but persons who wish to be served. Actually, a superior can serve only as she is allowed to serve, work only where she is permitted to work, and strengthen and sustain love in the community only in the measure that she is loved by the community. That this may be read backward as well as forward is only part of the enduring mystery of love. Thus, the sisters will be well served only by someone who really desires to serve them, helped only by one equipped to help them; and they will be able to love in the measure that they are loved.

And then there is compassion. "Let her [the abbess] console the afflicted. Likewise, let her be the last refuge of the troubled, lest if they should not find with her the remedies for health, the sickness of despair might overcome the weak" (Rule of Saint Clare). True consolation does not come from without. It requires a genuine entering-in to the area of another's suffering, even into that "another". This is hardly possible for someone who has not suffered herself. It is invariably one who has personally experienced weakness who is qualified to help the weak. God become Man could "bear our infirmities" and have empirical knowledge of hunger, thirst, fatigue. We may say that the superior needs in the psychological sense to become the suffering sister in order to bear the sister's infirmity.

It could be hazardous to have for superior one who has never been ill, never had a headache, never been embalmed by fatigue. Such a person could have only speculative knowledge of the depression, irritability, peevishness, and all that inglorious train which usually accompany physical infirmity. How much less can a superior be understanding of impatience, tension, frustration, insecurity, and the rest if she does not experience these destructive forces within herself? There is such a thing as a superior who is too serene, too detached, even—yes—too perfect. "To the weak I became weak that I might gain the weak" (1 Cor 9:22). It is good, probably necessary, possibly even essential that superiors be empowered to exercise compassion in that deeply relational manner of one who has herself known infirmity. And so God invariably sees to it that the office of superior carries with it a generous measure of humiliations that, rightly appreciated, may engender humility.

The group dynamics method of analyzing the superior's faults and shortcomings may seem a little amusing and certainly superfluous to superiors who have discovered that of all the charges they have ever held in religious life, that of being superior is unquestionably the most humiliating. What can make one so painfully aware of one's own spotted condition as to be commissioned to present other persons unspotted to God? What discovers so profoundly to a soul her own talent for taking the wrong direction as to be entrusted with the direction of others? But such humiliations are not only salutary for the superior, but contributive to the quality of her service to others. The person unaware of her own weakness will scarcely be compassionate to the weakness of others. And the person too strong to be weak is seldom the person to bring strength to the weak.

Happily, we all seem to be acutely aware these days of service being the office of the superior. We want, however, to carry Christ's idea of service to its limits. For he came not only "to serve", but "to give his life as a ransom for many". It is a lesson we must be repeatedly taught, but which brings superiors a unique consolation when it is remembered: that, especially for a sister weak in virtue or wavering in her vocation to high holiness, the superior must add to exhortation, to compassion, to correction, to appeal, the final measure of herself, which is suffering unto death. Sometimes the only way to reach a frustrated sister is to suffer the frustration of not being able to reach her. The best way to steady the insecure may be to suffer the insecurity of not knowing how to help them. There are many ways for the superior to offer her life as a ransom for her daughters, none of which allow her the repose of physical death.

"The last refuge of the troubled" is Saint Clare's description of the abbess. Refuge, place of shelter, warmth, security—these are functions proper to a mother. It is strange that in these days of accent on religious community as a family, we seem to be simultaneously rejecting any underscoring of "mother". What kind of family do we envision? A household of orphans? There is something very odd about the decrying in some quarters of the mother-daughter relationship as maternalism-infantilism. The implication would be that mothers never have daughters except in perambulators. Is it not true that mothers have grown daughters on whom they depend, who share their responsibilities, who suggest and advise? It is indeed ironic that in an age of such insistence on love rather than legalism, we should have become uneasy about the title of mother.

"Superiors should gladly listen to their subjects", counsels *Perfectae Caritatis* (no. 14). Saint Clare pointed out over seven centuries ago in that terse style she always employed when mentioning the obvious, "The Lord often reveals what is better to the lesser ones" (Rule of Saint Clare). That we are presently emphasizing the importance of the superior's listening to her sisters is not a matter of having discovered a new concept of superior-subject relationships, but may well be a matter of admitting we have sometimes failed to do what is obviously required if the superior is to "foster harmony among them for the good of the community and the Church" and "govern these as sons of God, respecting their human dignity" (PC, no. 14).

God reveals what is best not exclusively nor necessarily directly to the superior, but through a communal listening for his inspirations and a communal sharing of them. And the superior's duty "to decide and command" (ibid.) cannot be adequately, lovingly, or even intelligently discharged except by her attentiveness to the charisms God gives to subjects. But as the sisters help the superior by revealing to her what God has revealed to them, the superior in her turn must reveal something to the sisters. One thing she must constantly reveal is vocational identity.

In this period of greater care in screening subjects, it may be important to remember that superiors, too, need to be screened. Above all, with the help of the Holy Spirit, they need to screen themselves. We are anxious about the multiplying uncertainties and insecurity in religious communities. We have so many religious unsure of themselves, unsure of their place in the Church, unsure of the meaning of their vocation. There are various and complex reasons for this, but one reason not usually much dwelt upon in discussions is the unsureness of superiors. If they do not have a strong, sure, unshakable sense of *vocation*, it is inevitable that the community, too, will be riddled with anxiety and insecurity. Is it not to a deepening of our sense not only of personal identity but of communal identity that the Decree on the Adaptation and Renewal of Religious Life invites us? "The gifts which these communities possess differ according to the grace which is allotted to them" (PC, no. 8). The "members [in the Mystical Body of Christ] do not all have the same function (Rom. 12:4)" (PC, no. 7).

We live in a searching age. And a searcher is a very good sort of person to be. It is folly to pretend we have found the *fullness* of truth and recognized the boundaries of vocation, rather after the manner of a land surveyor. Actually, all religious are meant to be specialists in seeking the truth, which to them, as to the apostles before them, is revealed in the measure they have become capable of receiving it. "I have many things to tell you, but you cannot bear them now" (Jn 16:12). And it is radical to the meaning of vocation that it has no boundaries, is not static, and certainly is not rigid and inflexible. The same vocation is *expressed* differently in variant social milieus, chronologies, and even situations. Styles change not less in the expression of religious life than in literature, art, and architecture. But essence does not. And so an outstanding duty of the superior is to reveal to her sisters the essence of their common vocation. Obviously, she cannot do this if she does not know or is not sure what that essence is.

The oneness of the people of God is not ensured by the uncertainties of the members as to their own proper role in salvation history. Yet, it almost appears that identity crises are being accepted if not actually pursued by some as an enduring mode of expression. One cannot, however, live in crisis forever. You either have to die or get well. True, a third dreary choice would be to elect permanent invalidism.

To change the expression of a truth while preserving the integrity of truth, we must be absolutely sure of that truth and educated to deal with it. *Perfectae Caritatis* reminds us of this in various numbers and very strikingly in number 7, which deals with the cloistered communities entirely dedicated to contemplation: "Their manner of living should be revised according to the principles and criteria of adaptation and renewal mentioned above. However, their withdrawal from the world and the exercises proper to the contemplative life should be preserved with the utmost care." Contemplatives are thus urged in the Decree to be anchored in the truth that withdrawal from the world (a positive attitude opposed to a negative escapism or flight) is so radical to their vocation as to call for preservation "with the utmost care". Withdrawal they must understand as a face-on, backing-up process, the kind of thing one does to get a proper perspective for appraisal and appreciation. The turning of one's back on a thing and running *away* from it is a different procedure entirely and hardly praiseworthy if the thing involved is the world. It has nothing to do with withdrawal. So, understanding the meaning of withdrawal and with a clear knowledge of what the "exercises proper to the contemplative life" are, contemplatives are equipped to use the light of the Holy Spirit revealed in prayer and also in discussions and mutual sharing to revise "their manner of living".

This is only one example of a principle touching upon every form of religious life, a principle with which *Perfectae Caritatis* is thoroughly imbued. The kind of conviction it demands is a certainty not at all inconsistent with searching or with our universal state of becoming. And if the superior lacks this conviction and this basic certitude, it will not normally characterize her community, either.

It is delightful to discover how many of these fresh new concepts of community life are as old as our Order! "Medieval" Saint Clare condensed a workshopful of ideas on the accessibility, serviceability, and approachability of the superior in one paragraph of her Testament: "Let her also be so kind and courteous that they can confidently make known their needs and trustingly have recourse to her at any hour as it will seem to them profitable to do, both for themselves as for their sisters."

When we spread out that condensation, we have a considerable knowledge of what sisters need in a superior. She is to be courteous ("respecting their human dignity" [PC, no. 14]) and easy to get along with ("expressing . . . the love with which God loves their subjects" [ibid.]). Even the "master listener" of our present discovery would probably be allowed office hours, but Saint Clare invites her daughters to "trustingly have recourse to her at *any* hour". If that is not plain enough, she rephrases it: "as it will seem to them profitable to do". "Superiors should gladly listen to their subjects" (PC, no. 14). Clare insists that the abbess must do this any time at all that the sisters have something to say.

The sisters are to come to the superior "both for themselves as for their sisters" (Testament of Saint Clare). "Superiors should . . . foster harmony among them for the good of the community" (PC, no. 14). The Franciscan ideal envisioned by Saint Francis and entrusted by him to Saint

Clare had nothing at all of isolationism about it. There was no trace of the "me and my perfection" attitude at Rivo Torto or San Damiano. To have one's gaze fixed on God was not understood to mean letting one's companions shift for themselves.

But with all her emphasizing of humble service and accessibility as characteristic of a good superior, Saint Clare takes care to remind subjects that "[t]he sisters who are subject to authority ... should keep in mind that they have put aside their own wills for the Lord. Thus I will that they obey their Mother as they have promised the Lord of their own free will" (Testament of Saint Clare). She accents freedom, the freedom with which responsible religious women have decided to subordinate their wills and obey, ". . . so that their Mother, seeing the charity, humility, and unity which they have toward one another, may carry more lightly the whole burden of the office she bears and that which is vexing and bitter be turned into sweetness because of their holy living" (ibid.). Saint Clare was thus not above asking her sisters to help her, just as she wished to help them.

It was a strong family spirit that characterized early Franciscans. The ministering superiors even in the friaries were asked by Saint Francis to be "mothers" to their brothers. No wonder that the Decree on the Adaptation and Renewal of Religious Life urges us to return to the spirit of our founders.

AFTERWORD

In the more than forty years since the promulgation of *Perfectae Caritatis*, religious life has undergone many changes, all marked with a greater or lesser degree of success. "Time will tell where wisdom lies", our Lord remarked in the Gospels. And the practical results reaped in the past decades have surely distinguished genuine renewal conducive to growth from a specious counterfeit resulting in confusion, loss of identity, defection of members, and (taken to the ultimate extreme) the destruction of the religious institute. In retrospect, it is clear that where religious have kept the pursuit of perfect charity at the foreground of their strivings, rooting their efforts in the interior renewal and return to the sources advocated by the Council, the results have been predictably positive. Where they have rushed first into a flurry of external adaptations, the results here, too, have been predictable.

When Mother Mary Francis first penned her "marginals" on to the Decree on the Adaptation and Renewal of the Religious Life, she could hardly have foreseen all of the consequences, either of the document or of her own reflections upon it. More than forty years and six daughterhouses later, our Roswell community remains grateful for her clarity of vision and unfailing courage, which guided our community so securely through the post-Conciliar era. Loyalty to the Church, fidelity to her directives, love for her Franciscan vocation and a radical commitment to it, a practical idealism that began and ended with the Gospel—these were some of the qualities that had characterized her leadership and which we cherish as part of her legacy. At the dawn of the millennium it is our joy and privilege to share this legacy once again with all our brothers and sisters, praying that through these pages they may once again recover the vision for the renewal of their own religious life.